THE PULITZER PRIZE NOVELS
A Critical Backward Look

The

PULITZER
PRIZE
NOVELS

A Critical
Backward Look

BY W. J. STUCKEY

UNIVERSITY OF OKLAHOMA PRESS : NORMAN

LIBRARY OF CONGRESS CATALOG CARD NUMBER: 66–10295

Copyright 1966 by the University of Oklahoma Press, Publishing Division of the University. Composed and printed at Norman, Oklahoma, U.S.A., by the University of Oklahoma Press. First edition, March, 1966; second printing, September, 1966; third printing, June, 1968.

For June

Preface

WHEN I BEGAN to prepare this account of the Pulitzer prize novel, I wrote to the grandson of Joseph Pulitzer explaining what I proposed to do and asking his assistance in obtaining permission to examine the records of the juries and the Advisory Board of the Graduate School of Journalism at Columbia University. In reply, Mr. Pulitzer advised me to write to Professor John Hohenberg, executive secretary of the Advisory Board, and also to Carl W. Ackerman, dean emeritus of the Graduate School of Journalism, which I did. Dean Ackerman answered that he could not permit anyone to examine his private files. Miss Frances M. Barry, administrative assistant to Edward Barrett, dean of the School, replied for Professor Hohenberg, who was on sabbatical leave. Miss Barry wrote that in Professor Hohenberg's absence my letter had been referred to Dean Barrett, who was temporarily out of the country. Miss Barry said that on Dean Barrett's return, I might expect an answer to my request. No further word came, however, and after a time, I wrote Dean Barrett himself, repeating the request I had made earlier to Professor Hohenberg. When neither Dean Barrett nor Miss Barry replied to my second letter, it became apparent that if I were to find out anything about the administration of the Pulitzer novel prize, I would have to do so without the assistance of the Columbia authorities.

In the early years of the Pulitzer prizes, Columbia University officials were not so secretive as they were later to become. During the 1920's, announcements made by Nicholas Murray Butler, president of Columbia, and statements attributed to some of the jurors were reported by the newspapers. From these reports and announcements it has been possible to assemble a picture of what, at one time, went on behind the scenes. Since 1929, however, the Columbia officials have made few official announcements to the newspapers about the system by which the Pulitzer prize winners are selected. Consequently the section of this study which deals with the method of selection is sketchy and often conjectural. It may be, for example, that the juries do not have as much power as I attribute to them, or that the Advisory Board is now more active than it used to be. These tentative judgments will have to stand, however, until the Pulitzer authorities decide to put the record straight.

Interesting as it would be to know how and, especially, why certain books were awarded Pulitzer prizes, the administrative procedure of the Pulitzer authorities is not the main concern here. The main focus of this book is the prize novels themselves—their themes, ideas, sentiments, and especially their art and lack of art. The approach is, therefore, chiefly critical. Since the Pulitzer prize novels are not all of the same technical accomplishment and intellectual sophistication, I have avoided following a set procedure in my analyses. Instead, I have taken the approach that seemed most appropriate to each work. While maneuvering in this way, I have nevertheless kept in mind a set of general standards which, it seems to me, are basic to contemporary conceptions of serious fiction. Structurally, a novel should be coherent. Plot, style, characters, and tone should all contribute toward the central effect of the book. On the simplest level this means that what is said in one part of the novel should not contradict what is said in another. At a higher level one might think of this requirement as "organic structure"—vehicle and theme should merge and be indistinguishable. The theme ought not to be imposed on the material, but should grow— or seem to grow—out of the material itself. Actions and dialogue ought to create, not illustrate, character. And characters ought not to act out "ideas."

On the intellectual level, a novel—a serious novel, that is—ought to take into account the complexity of life. It ought not, in other words, to offer a simple formula which seems to explain or sum up the whole of human nature and experience. Further, attitudes appropriate to moral tracts, though useful perhaps in instructing the young, are not appropriate to novels intended for mature readers. A serious novel explores the implications of the characters and situations with which it deals; it goes beyond mere appearances, and, in fact, sometimes alters the reader's preconceptions of reality.

In the following chapters of critical analysis, I deal to some extent with all of the novels to which Pulitzer prizes were given between 1917 and 1962. I do not, however, treat each novel at the same length. Those that are well written or interesting within the Pulitzer tradition I deal with rather thoroughly. Novels that lie completely outside the domain of serious fiction (such as John Hersey's A Bell for Adano) I treat very briefly.

Literary criticism, at last, even when well buttressed by analyses or by the judgments of others, depends ultimately upon personal impressions. What a critic finds in a novel will depend in large part upon what he is prepared to look for, and as much as he may wish to be objective, it is inevitable that he should be influenced by his own preferences and by those of the critics and novelists he has read and admired. Without wishing to shift responsibility for my critical standards, then, I should like to mention a few of the works to which I feel particularly indebted: "The Art of Fiction," by Henry James; *The Craft of Fiction*, by Percy Lubbock; *Forms of Modern Fiction*, edited by William Van O'Connor; *The American Renaissance*, by F. O. Matthiessen; *Fiction and the Reading Public*, by Q. D. Leavis; *The House of Fiction*, by Caroline Gordon and Allen Tate; and *English Prose Style*, by Sir Herbert Read.

One final prefatory comment: Some readers will doubtless feel that the approach I have taken in this study is unreasonable, that I am attempting to judge what are, for the most part, works of popular entertainment by standards that can be applied only to literary masterpieces. My answer to such objections would be this: In designating the prize novels as "the best" or as "a distinguished novel of the year," the Pulitzer authorities have, in a sense, taken the matter out of my hands. Their position clearly implies that, as one Pulitzer juror put it, these novels are thought to be books "not just for a year but for many years to come."[1] And so, to have treated the Pulitzer novels simply as the artifacts of popular sub-culture that many of them are would have been to beg the question that a study of this kind must answer: How distinguished are Pulitzer prize novels?

Finally, I should like to thank all those persons who have assisted me, directly and indirectly, in the writing of this book. I wish especially to thank Professor Guy A. Cardwell of Washington University, who first suggested that the

[1] The *New York Times*, May 17, 1929, p. 12.

book needed to be written. His interest and encouragement, as well as his guidance and incisive criticism, were of immeasurable assistance both in the conception and in the initial writing. I am also deeply indebted to Professor Sarah Youngblood of the University of Minnesota and to Mrs. Margaret Bolsterli for reading large portions of the manuscript and making suggestions for stylistic revisions. To my colleague, Professor C. E. Nelson, I owe a special thanks. He went over the final manuscript in its entirety and gave it an astute and sympathetic reading. Because of his criticisms, the central issue in this book has been brought into sharper focus. Last, I wish to express my gratitude to the Purdue Research Foundation for awarding me a grant so that I might have time free to write and put this book in its final form.

My most personal debt is to my wife. Without her encouragement and active assistance, this work would not have been possible.

W. J. STUCKEY

West Lafayette, Indiana
December 10, 1965

Contents

xiii

THE PULITZER PRIZE NOVELS
A Critical Backward Look

CHAPTER ONE

Joseph Pulitzer and His Prizes

T HE LIFE STORY of Joseph Pul-
itzer, founder of the Pulitzer prizes in journalism, letters,
and music, fits beautifully into a familiar pattern of American
success. He arrived in this country in 1864 at the age of
seventeen, without money and with almost no knowledge of
the English language. But by a combination of hard work,
shrewdness, thrift, perseverance, some luck, and some opportunism, he made his way relentlessly to financial eminence
in his profession. When he died in 1911, Joseph Pulitzer left
a fortune of almost nineteen million dollars, including two
large and prosperous newspapers, the St. Louis *Post-Dispatch*
and the New York *World*.[1]

Like some other self-made millionaires, Joseph Pulitzer
has also left behind an ambiguous reputation as both an
exploiter and a benefactor of the American public. And even
by sympathetic critics Pulitzer has been charged with helping
debase the standards of American journalism—through
stunts, sensationalism, and means otherwise catering to the
taste of the masses.[2] But Pulitzer himself seemed to have
felt that in the conduct of his newspapers he had been a

[1] Don C. Seitz, *Joseph Pulitzer: His Life & Letters* (New York, 1924).
[2] Frank Luther Mott, *American Journalism* (New York, 1941),
430–45.

3

model of integrity. For despite what might seem to more objective observers as a deliberate courting of the lowest taste, Pulitzer evidently felt that in turning out a "cheap," "bright," and interesting newspaper, he was giving the people something that would otherwise have been denied them. The profits he made from the pennies of the poor were not just so much money in the bank. They were a return on public services. In his newspaper columns and feature articles, he brought news down to the people's level; on his editorial pages he took issue with the "purse potentates" and battled for the people with "earnest sincerity."[3]

Whatever Pulitzer's deepest motives may have been and whatever his severest critics may have thought these were, his devotion to the interests of the common people and his own self-interest were, in his mind, inseparable. Though rich and successful himself, he despised the privileged classes and still emotionally identified himself with the poor and the disenfranchised, a class to which his early poverty and immigrant status had consigned him. Pulitzer was also a moral pragmatist. That is, he knew from practical experience that to expand and prosper in mid-nineteenth-century America, a newspaper had to be not only cheap and popular, it had to be "morally" sound. Without morals, he once wrote, no newspaperman can hope to succeed.[4] If this seems crass and hypocritical, it is also common sensical in the tradition of Ben Franklin.

While he was still a fairly young man, Pulitzer's health failed and he had to surrender direct management of his newspapers to subordinates. Although he continued to keep in touch, receiving reports and issuing commands by telegram or cable, he now had time for other things, including

[3] Mott, *American Journalism*, 434.
[4] Seitz, *Joseph Pulitzer*, 447.

the disposition of his fortune and the establishment of several endowments, including one for his favorite project, a journalism college. The establishment of such a school, Pulitzer felt, would raise the standards of American newspapers and put journalists on somewhat the same footing as doctors and lawyers. He did not mean to make scholars or intellectuals of apprentice journalists, of course, but only to give them enough history, law, literature, and morality to help them carry on their careers successfully.[5] In 1890, Pulitzer approached Harvard University with an offer of one million dollars if the university would undertake sponsorship of his school. The offer was turned down by President Eliot. Two years later, Pulitzer made a similar proposal to Columbia University, and it was also rejected by President Low and the university's trustees.[6]

Off and on for another ten years, Pulitzer brooded over his project, revising, polishing, and attempting to make it more acceptable to the academic world. Then in 1903 he submitted a revised plan to Columbia University's new president, Nicholas Murray Butler. President Butler, as it turned out, was more sympathetic to the idea of a college of journalism. This time the Columbia trustees accepted the one million dollars and undertook to establish Joseph Pulitzer's school.[7] Then, while public announcements were being prepared, Pulitzer began negotiations with Columbia for the establishment of another favorite project, a series of annual prizes and scholarships in journalism and letters. To persuade the trustees to undertake this additional responsibility, Pulitzer offered to add another million dollars to the endowment of the new journalism school—provided that half the

[5] Joseph Pulitzer, "The College of Journalism," N. Amer. Rev., Vol. CLXXVIII (May, 1904), 641–80.
[6] Seitz, Joseph Pulitzer, 436.
[7] Ibid., 445.

income from this additional million would be given away each year as cash prizes in journalism and letters. This second million with its attendant responsibilities was also accepted by Columbia, and establishment of the Pulitzer prizes was thereby assured.[8]

In his negotiations with Columbia, Pulitzer displayed some of the same stubbornness that had characterized many of his dealings with subordinates on the *World*. He was willing to put his journalism college and yearly prizes into Columbia's control, but he wished to make certain that they would be managed according to his specifications.[9] Although he was too ill himself to take a hand in setting up the journalism school, he made certain that its initial character was shaped by journalistic rather than academic minds: He arranged with Columbia for the creation of an Advisory Board, to be appointed by himself, to help launch his college and to take charge of the prizes in letters and journalism.

Although Pulitzer gave this board the authority to determine the standards of excellence to be looked for in the prize-winning works, he could not forbear stipulating the standards by which he wanted the board to be guided. The intent of these terms as Pulitzer set them down was quite explicit, though the meaning was exceedingly vague:

> Annually, for the American novel published during the year which shall best present the wholesome atmosphere of American life and the highest standard of American manners and manhood. $1,000.
>
> Annually, for the original American play performed in New York which shall best present the educational value of the stage in raising the standard of good morals, good taste, and good manners. $1,000.

[8] *Ibid.*, 445–48.
[9] *Ibid.*, 453–60.

Annually, for the best book of the year upon the history of the United States. $2,000.

Annually, for the best American biography teaching patriotic and unselfish service to the people, illustrated by an eminent example, excluding as too obvious the names of Washington and Abraham Lincoln. $1,000.[10]

Since the Advisory Board was composed mainly of newspaper editors and publishers, it could have made little real difference whether the board set up its own standards or tried to follow Pulitzer's. For the board was given the responsibility of performing a function for which its members were not professionally trained: to assess the merits of the hundreds of novels, plays, biographies, and histories published each year. Whoever designed the prize-awarding procedure recognized this, and some time before the first awards were granted, it was arranged for juries of literary "experts" to make these decisions behind the scenes. The Advisory Board's power was further curtailed by the fact that although Pulitzer's will explicitly gave it sole authority to select the prize-winning works, the decisions of the Board are subject to automatic review by the trustees of Columbia University. Any award voted by the Advisory Board, before it can become valid, then, must be approved by the university administration. Although the trustees themselves have evidently not intervened in these decisions, high officials of Columbia University, using the authority of the trustees' veto power over the Advisory Board, have interfered at least on one occasion and probably on others as well.

As to who actually controls the Pulitzer prize decisions,

[10] Pulitzer's biographers are not in agreement about which prizes he specified in his will. See Seitz, *Joseph Pulitzer*, 463–64, James Wyman Barrett, *Joseph Pulitzer and His World* (New York, 1941), 262, and also *New York Times*, June 4, 1918, p. 7. Seitz includes the poetry prize as among those specified by Pulitzer; Barrett and the *Times* account do not.

7

it is not easy to say. In the early years an attempt was made to dissociate Columbia University from the prizes. In 1925, for instance, President Nicholas Murray Butler was quoted as having said that aside from handling the funds for the Pulitzer awards, the university had nothing to do with selecting the yearly winners.[11] As the years passed, however, and the university became increasingly sensitive to the public relations value of the prize, the general impression created by official announcements was that Columbia was very much in control of the Pulitzer prizes. And during the years that Butler was president of Columbia and ex officio chairman of the Advisory Board, it seems that he carefully scrutinized all of the recommendations of the Advisory Board before he sent them on to the trustees for final approval. It was he who forced the board to withdraw the novel prize it voted to give Ernest Hemingway's *For Whom the Bell Tolls*, in 1941.[12] The indications are that he kept the prize from going to other works as well. But whether or not President Butler directly interfered in many other decisions, the knowledge that he would review all nominations may have made the jurors (some of whom were Columbia faculty members) as well as members of the Advisory Board unduly cautious in their decisions. Indeed, it is quite likely that the university's concern for its public image has had more to do with the kind of fiction the Advisory Board and its jurors have selected for the prize than the naïve standards that Joseph Pulitzer bequeathed to his literary executors.

Considering the time at which Pulitzer formulated his standards, it is not surprising to find him identifying literary excellence with moral high-mindedness. For although the

[11] *New York Times*, March 30, 1925, p. 5.
[12] See Arthur Krock, "In the Nation," *New York Times*, May 11, 1962, p. 30, and page 123 below.

best American novelists and critics of the period would not have agreed, it was widely assumed by most Victorian critics and writers that the best literature was explicitly moralistic. It will be recalled from Henry James's famous essay, "The Art of Fiction," that Walter Besant listed as one of the chief requirements for the novel a "conscious moral purpose."[13] Pulitzer's moralism, of course, went far beyond even Besant's. The phrase "conscious moral purpose" admits the possibility of a writer's including in his novel both "bad" and "good" characters, whereas Pulitzer's phrases "presenting the wholesome atmosphere of American life" and the "highest standards of American manners and manhood" suggest that only books fit for a Sunday school library qualified for a Pulitzer fiction prize. Certainly Hawthorne's *The Scarlet Letter*, Melville's *Moby Dick*, Twain's *Huckleberry Finn*, or Crane's *The Red Badge of Courage* could not have qualified. Nor could James's *The Ambassadors*, nor, technically, even Howells' *The Rise of Silas Lapham*, which comes closer to fulfilling the spirit of Pulitzer's conditions than any other important American novel published during Pulitzer's lifetime.[14]

As naïve as Pulitzer's standards were, they could not have caused much difficulty in the 1880's or even in the early 1900's. But after 1917, the year the first prizes were awarded, American literature came to mirror and often encourage the social revolution that was sweeping away the code of polite behavior that governed the public lives of middle-class Americans—a generally accepted standard that might have given Pulitzer's terms some semblance of meaning. In fact, the success of much of the new fiction—John

[13] Henry James, "The Art of Fiction," *The House of Fiction*, ed. by Leon Edel (London, 1957), 42.

[14] Pulitzer, perhaps, was translating into literary terms his notion of what would be appropriate for newspaper readers.

Dos Passos' *Three Soldiers,* Sinclair Lewis' *Main Street,* F. Scott Fitzgerald's *This Side of Paradise,* and Ernest Hemingway's *The Sun Also Rises*—was to depend in part upon the reader's awareness that the standards of conventional morality were being questioned. By 1925 the criteria set down by Pulitzer for the guidance of his administrators were irrelevant even to second- and third-rate American novels.

It is to Joseph Pulitzer's credit that although he left his administrators a set of hopelessly unworkable literary standards, he did give them the authority to set themselves free: Pulitzer's will provided that any of the conditions he had drawn up for the granting of these prizes could be changed by the Advisory Board when rendered necessary by the passing of time or if such changes or alterations seemed "conducive to the public good."[15] In 1928, after having awarded only eleven prizes, the board used these powers to alter the official terms for the literature prizes. The results, however, were not much more satisfactory. The first change, made in 1928, stipulated that the novel prize would be given "for the

[15] Barrett, *Joseph Pulitzer and His World,* 264.

[16] Robert Morss Lovett, "Pulitzer Prize," *New Republic,* Vol. LX (Sept. 11, 1929), 100–101, and *New York Times,* May 13, 1930, p. 1. This account of the changes made in the terms of the novel award may not be accurate, for newspaper reports of the time are confusing and contradictory. For example, when *Laughing Boy* was given the prize in 1930, it was reported that the official terms were for the novel "which best presents the whole atmosphere of American life." (See *New York Times,* May 13, 1930, p. 1.) A year or so later, however, it was reported that the award to *Laughing Boy* was "for the best American novel published during the year, preferably one which shall best present the wholesome atmosphere of American life." (*New York Times,* Nov. 18, 1931, p. 25.) When the 1931 awards were announced, it was merely stated that *Years of Grace* was judged "the year's best novel." Then in November, 1931, F. D. Fackenthal, an official of Columbia University, was quoted as saying that "last spring" (presumably at the annual May meeting), the Advisory Board decided to change the conditions "simply as a matter of clarity," and that the award "this year (1932?) will be for 'the best novel published during the year by an American author.'" (*New York Times,* May 5, 1931, p. 1 and November 18, 1931, p. 25.)

American novel published during the year, preferably one which shall best present the whole atmosphere of American life."[16] The Advisory Board had dispensed with the "uplift" requirements, but had retained some of the old phraseology and mixed it together with some vagaries of its own. What was intended by *the* American novel and by the *whole* atmosphere of American life? Did the authorities mean that in order to qualify for a Pulitzer prize a novel had to get *all* of American life into one novel? Or did *whole* simply mean that it might include the sordid as well as the wholesome aspects of American life—whatever these might be?

The following year, evidently in an attempt to clear up the confusion, the authorities announced that they had formulated another new set of requirements for the novel: The Pulitzer prize in 1930 would be given for "the best American novel published during the year, preferably one which shall best present the wholesome atmosphere of American life."[17] These new conditions, which read like a statement of compromise between literary critics and public moralists, were certainly more precise than the last version. However, by retaining the equivocal adverb "preferably," the authorities seem to acknowledge that the "best" American novel might not be wholesome, which could hardly have pleased the moralists. And so the next year, 1931, the Pulitzer authorities announced a third set of conditions. These came out unequivocally for excellence as the only official criterion for the fiction prize. The Pulitzer novel prize would now be given "for the best novel" published during the year by an American author.[18] However, this forthright declaration for quality was evidently inspired less by the authorities' desire to make excellence their only criterion than by their

[17] *New York Times*, May 14, 1929, p. 14.
[18] *Ibid.*, Nov. 18, 1931, p. 25.

fondness for Pearl Buck's best seller, *The Good Earth*, a novel set in China.

But more changes were to come. So much controversy was stirred up in 1934 when the Pulitzer officials rejected their drama jury's vote for Maxwell Anderson's play, *Mary of Scotland*—jurors were resigning and denouncing the Pulitzer officials in print and on the radio—that the authorities again altered the conditions of the literature awards, the novel as well as the drama awards, giving preference once more to American material. Henceforth, the novel prize would be given "for the best novel published during the year by an American author, preferably dealing with American life."[19]

The critics were not silenced, however. One disaffected drama juror, Clayton Hamilton, continued to attack the drama selections and, in 1935, disgruntled New York drama critics founded a rival drama prize, the New York Drama Critics Circle Award.[20] In an obvious attempt to put a stop to such criticism, or to cut the ground from under their critics' feet, Pulitzer authorities in 1936 made a fifth change in the official prize conditions. Instead of claiming to select the "best" novel [play, etc.] of the year, they would now simply give their prize to "a distinguished novel of the year."[21] The new terms, of course, amounted to little more than word-juggling. The fact that the Pulitzer officials continued to single out one work from the hundreds produced each year implied (whether they wished to admit it or not) that, for reasons unspecified, the chosen work was thought to be the best one published in that year.

Since 1936 one more alteration has been made in the

[19] *Ibid.*, May 12, 1934, p. 27.
[20] Clayton Hamilton, "Poor Pulitzer Prize." *Amer. Mercury*, Vol. XXXV (May, 1935), 25–32; *New York Times*, May 7, 1935, p. 21, and May 5, 1936, p. 18.
[21] *New York Times*, May 7, 1936, p. 21.

official terms under which the novel award is made. In 1947 the word "novel" was dropped and the phrase "fiction in book form" was substituted.[22] These are the terms under which the awards have since been made. Considering the many fine collections of short stories that have appeared in this country since 1917—by Ring Lardner, F. Scott Fitzgerald, Ernest Hemingway, Caroline Gordon, Katherine Anne Porter, and many others—this change was long overdue. Regrettably enough, the Pulitzer authorities appear to have been motivated less by a desire to broaden the scope of the award than to accommodate a poorly written collection of journalistic sketches that could not qualify under the old conditions: James A. Michener's *Tales of the South Pacific*.[23]

One other change made in Pulitzer's will is worth noting. Sometime during 1941 or early 1942 the monetary value of the novel prize was reduced from $1,000 to $500. No official announcement of the change was made at the time and no explanation was afterward given. The reason, it seems, was clearly revealed when the newspapers carried an account of the 1942 prize winners. The cash value of all of the literary prizes was reduced from a total of $6,000 to $2,500; the value of the journalism prizes was increased from $2,000 to $7,500.

During the early 1920's, when the Pulitzer prize was not well known and officials of Columbia University wished the public to understand that the prize works were being selected by highly qualified people, some information about the prize selection procedure was revealed to the public through the newspapers. It was explained that the Pulitzer prizes were

[22] *Ibid.*, May 11, 1947, p. 45.
[23] See Chap. VII below.

13

awarded as the result of a "national competition" in which writers from all parts of the United States competed. In order to enter a book in the contest, novelists or their agents (i.e., their publishers) had only to submit a letter of nomination and a copy of the book to the Pulitzer authorities. The novels so nominated were then read by a three-man jury of "experts" who met together, nominated the prize-winning work, and passed on their recommendation to the Advisory Board of the School of Journalism. The board, at its annual meeting in May, then voted to accept or reject the recommendations of its juries and passed on its decisions to the trustees of Columbia University for approval and official certification.[24]

Official announcements made during this period also let it be known that the men who served on the Pulitzer juries were chosen from among the members of two national literary organizations, the American Academy of Arts and Letters (of which Nicholas Murray Butler was president) and the National Institute of Arts and Letters. The actual method of selecting jurors, the term of office, and the operation of the juries, however, has never been explained by the Pulitzer authorities. The little information we have about these matters has been revealed unofficially—usually by jurors. Judging from this rather sketchy evidence, the judges for all of the juries that assist the Advisory Board in selecting the prize-winning works are (or, at one time, were) chosen from a list of "qualified" people prepared by the secretaries of the American Academy and the National Institute.[25] Appointment was for one year, though it appears that the same

24 New York Times, Nov. 27, 1921, p. 3.
25 See A[my] L[oveman], "The Pulitzer Awards," Sat. Rev., Vol. XXXIV (May 19, 1951), 22–23, and a letter from Carl W. Ackerman, Sat. Rev., Vol. XXXIV (July 14, 1951), 26. See also New York Times, May 6, 1962, p. 135.

persons frequently served several years on the novel jury, or sometimes alternated between juries, perhaps serving on both the drama and the novel juries.

After the jury was appointed, each member was apparently provided with a list of the novels that had been formally "nominated" by the authors or for them, usually by their publishers, and the process of narrowing the field began. After the committee had eliminated all works that were thought ineligible and had narrowed the field to three novels the jury members could agree were the best candidates, a final vote took place. Each juror ranked the candidates in the order of his preference and sent his ballot to the chairman of the jury, who then totaled the results (giving three points for a first place vote, two for a second, etc.) and forwarded to Columbia the name of the candidate that had received the largest number of points. At its annual meeting in May, the Advisory Board then voted on the recommendations of its juries.[26] This nominating procedure was in effect (officially, at least) from 1918 until 1934, when, because of the public dispute with the drama jurors, a new system was officially instituted. Beginning in 1934, all literature juries were instructed not to recommend one candidate for the prize, but instead to submit the names of several possible candidates along with the jury's reasons for recommending each one. The final decision was then to be made by the Advisory Board.[27]

The names of Pulitzer novel jurors were never officially revealed by Columbia University. However, in the 1920's, when the prize decisions were beginning to stir up contro-

[26] Hamilton, "Poor Pulitzer Prize," *Amer. Mercury*, Vol. XXXV (May, 1935), 25–32, and Robert Morss Lovett, "Pulitzer Prize," *New Republic*, Vol. XXVII (June 22, 1921), 114.

[27] *New York Times*, May 12, 1934, p. 17.

versy, President Butler offered the assurance that the men who served on the Pulitzer juries were "invariably men of the highest competence and reputation."[28] More recently, in 1951, in a letter to the editors of the *Saturday Review*, Carl W. Ackerman, then dean of Columbia's journalism school, in explaining why the names of Pulitzer jurors could not be made public, revealed that the jurors were all faculty members of prominent universities.[29] Other than these general assurances about the qualifications of the Pulitzer jurors, the public has never been told exactly who is responsible for selecting the prize works.

In the early years, before criticism of the awards put the authorities on the defensive, the names of jurors were sometimes leaked to the press. And jurors themselves occasionally made public statements about the awards. As a consequence, it has been possible to establish the identity of nine men who served on the novel juries between 1920 and 1928 and of one man who served in 1936. This is a small sampling, but it does give us an idea of the kind of men who have had a hand in making a number of Pulitzer awards.

Of these ten novel jurors, possibly the most interesting was Samuel McChord Crothers, a Unitarian minister and essayist who believed that the English novel had reached its highest development under Fielding and Richardson.[30] Crothers helped keep Sinclair Lewis' *Babbitt* from getting

[28] *Ibid.*, March 30, 1925, p. 5.

[29] Vol. XXXIV (July 14, 1951), 26.

[30] A sample of Crother's critical prose further illustrates his sensibility. "The poet," he wrote, "differs from the novelist in that he requires us to rest from our labors. The ordinary novel is easy reading, because it takes us as we are, in the midst of our hurry. . . . The great thing is still action, and we eagerly turn the pages to see what is going to happen next—unless we are reading some of our modern realistic studies of character. . . . But when we turn to the poets, we are in the land of the lotus-eaters . . . . The atmosphere is that of a perfect day." *The Gentle Reader* (Boston and New York, 1903), 46–47.

the prize in 1923—as did Jefferson Butler Fletcher, professor of comparative literature at Columbia, whose interest was the Italian Renaissance.[31] A somewhat more sympathetic juror was Robert Grant. In his younger days Grant had written several novels, and though his fictional talent was limited, he did qualify, technically, as an expert in fiction.[32] At the time Robert Grant served on the novel juries, he had long since abandoned a literary career and was a judge in the Massachusetts state courts. He served on the novel jury that withheld the prize in 1920 rather than give it to Joseph Hergesheimer's *Java Head* because presumably the book was not sufficiently wholesome.[33] Edwin Lefèvre also had written fiction, though his writing was possibly even less distinguished than Grant's: he wrote a kind of wooden cashbox romance in the tradition of Horatio Alger.[34] Lefèvre served on the jury that turned down *Boston*, Upton Sinclair's novel about the Sacco-Vanzetti case, because it was "too social-

[31] Books by Fletcher include *The Religion of Beauty in Women, and Other Essays on Platonic Love in Poetry and Society* (New York, 1911); *Dante* (Home University of Modern Knowledge, New York, 1916); *The Divine Comedy of Dante Alighieri*, trans. (New York, 1931).

[32] Among Grant's books are *Jack Hall* (Boston, 1888); *Jack in the Bush* (New York, 1893); *The Reflections of a Married Man* (New York, 1892); *The Opinions of a Philosopher* (New York, 1893); *Unleavened Bread* (New York, 1900), a novel about Selma, a social climber from the Middle West, which Hamlin Garland characterized, "a good book with sociological significance . . . true and broad-minded" (*My Friendly Contemporaries* [New York, 1932], 362); *The High Priestess* (New York, 1915); *Occasional Verses, 1873–1923* (Boston, 1926).

[33] *The Life and Letters of Stuart P. Sherman*, ed. by Jacob Zeitlin and Homer Woodbridge (2 vols. New York, 1929), II, 400.

[34] According to *Who Was Who in America, 1943–1950* (II, 317), Lefèvre studied engineering at Lehigh University, was "in journalism." His publications include *Wall Street Stories* (New York, 1901); *H. R.* (New York and London, 1915); *The Plunderers* (New York, 1916); *To the Last Penny* (New York and London, 1917); *Reminiscences of A Stock Operator* (New York, 1923).

17

istic" and voted instead for John Oliver's case study of an unfrocked Episcopalian priest, *Victim and Victor*.[35]

Richard Burton, a newspaper editor, head of the English Department at the University of Minnesota, and lecturer on contemporary fiction at the University of Chicago and Columbia University, was chairman of the jury that turned down *Boston*.[36] Burton's qualifications seem more impressive, but his pronouncements on fiction are for the most part an unsophisticated mixture of moralism and sentimental patriotism. Burton wrote, for example, that E. N. Westcott's *David Harum*, a sentimental best seller of the late 1890's, had a "remarkable and deserved popularity" because of the character of David.[37] And on another occasion, Burton declared that the fiction writers of the nineteenth century were too much preoccupied with technique at the expense of thought and character.[38] He also said that the chief function of American fiction is to teach

the different parts of the land to know each other and so to realize the variety and vastitude of our national life . . . . The novel, in this thought, is a mighty civilizer, drawing men together as do the wonderful material uses of electricity, and for the higher purposes of a comprehensive sympathy and love.[39]

Among the remaining five jurors were three men who

[35] *New York Times*, April 17, 1929, p. 5.

[36] Burton (who also served on the jury that gave the 1927 prize to Louis Bromfield for *Early Autumn*) was at one time managing editor of *The Churchman*; literary editor of the Hartford *Courant*; head of the English Department of the University of Minnesota, 1898–1902, 1906–25; lecturer on literature at Columbia, 1921–33. He served on Pulitzer juries in drama, poetry, fiction, and biography from 1920 to 1940. Among his published works are *Literary Leaders of America* (New York, 1903), lectures for the Chautauqua Society, and *Forces in Fiction and Other Essays* (Indianapolis, 1902).

[37] *Forces in Fiction and Other Essays*, 13.

[38] *Literary Leaders of America*, 202.

[39] *Ibid.*, 314.

had in their day rather considerable reputations as authorities on contemporary literature: Bliss Perry, Robert Morss Lovett, and Stuart Pratt Sherman. Bliss Perry was at one time editor of the *Atlantic Monthly* (1899–1909) and also professor of English at Princeton (1893–1900) and Harvard (1907–30). Professor Perry was also rather well known for his textbook, *A Study of Prose Fiction*, and for several other works on American literature.[40] Robert Morss Lovett was briefly an editor of the *New Republic* (1921), for a long time professor of English at Chicago (1904–36), and the author of books on Edith Wharton and on the contemporary novel, though he was probably best known as the co-editor of a history of English literature.[41] Stuart Pratt Sherman, the youngest of these three jurors, was probably the most widely known. He left his professorship at the University of Illinois to become editor of the book section of the New York *Herald-Tribune* in 1924 where he established a reputation as a highbrow interpreter of contemporary literature and an authority on culture.[42]

In his survey of the Pulitzer prize record, Arthur

[40] Other publications by Perry include: *Walt Whitman: His Life and Work* (Boston and New York, 1906); *The American Mind* (Boston and New York, 1912); *The American Spirit in Literature* (New Haven, 1918); *A Study of Poetry* (Boston and New York, 1920); *Emerson Today* (Princeton, 1931); *And Gladly Teach* (Boston and New York, 1935).

[41] Books by Lovett include: *Edith Wharton* (New York, 1925); *Preface to Fiction* (Chicago, 1931); and with William Vaughan Moody, *A History of English Literature* (New York, Chicago, and Boston, 1902). He also published two novels, *Richard Gresham* (New York, 1904), and *A Wingéd Victory* (New York, 1907). Lovett's autobiography, *All Our Years*, was published in 1948. In 1919 he was editor of the *Dial* and from 1922 to 1930 he was on the editorial board of the *New Republic*.

[42] Among Sherman's publications are: *On Contemporary Literature* (New York, 1917); *The Genius of America; Studies in Behalf of the Younger Generation* (New York, 1923); *Points of View* (New York, 1924); *The Main Stream* (New York, 1927). For an estimate of Sherman as a critic see Carl Van Doren, "The Great and the Good Tradition," *Many Minds* (New York, 1924), 67–82.

Mizener has suggested that the Pulitzer judges probably do know which are the best novels published each year but fail to select them because they contain offensive social, political, or moral sentiments.[43] It may be that jurors in later years have shied away from the best books because they have been too controversial, but those jurors who were serving in the 1920's did not seem to be worried about such things.[44] In their critical pronouncements, at least, the jurors did not make the kind of distinction between artistic merit and respectability that Mr. Mizener feels accounts for so many omissions from the Pulitzer roster. For Perry, Lovett, Sherman, and, no doubt, many of their colleagues, literary excellence and social usefulness were inseparably related. For example, in *The American Mind*, written in 1912, Bliss Perry argues that the period of rugged individualism is over in the United States and that a new era of socialism is dawning. This is not to say that the individual will be dispensed with, of course, but rather that there must now be a new and proper blending of individualism with fellowship, a mystical union in which, Perry says,

> we shall not forget the distinction between "each" and "all," but "all" will increasingly be placed at the service of "each." With fellowship based upon individualism, and with individualism ever leading to fellowship, America will perform its vital tasks, and its literature will be the unconscious and beautiful utterance of its inner life.[45]

[43] "Pulitzer Prizes," *Atlantic Monthly*, Vol. CC (July, 1957), 42–45.

[44] Also, at the time Lewis turned down the prize for *Arrowsmith*, it was reported in the *New York Times* (May 6, 1926, p. 17) that "someone familiar with the work of the Advisory Board" had said, "There had always been a tacit understanding that the prize should go each year to the best novel of the year, judged by a literary standard and that the implications of a moral standard had always been ignored."

[45] Pages 248–49.

Perry's evaluations of American literature were based on the assumption that since literature is an expression of the culture out of which it comes, genuinely American literature ought to reflect the "typical" qualities of the American people: It ought to be democratic, optimistic, idealistic, and "fundamentally wholesome." Perry realized, he said, that there might be a "leveling down instead of a leveling up. . . . You begin by recognizing the rights of the majority. You end by believing that the majority must be right."[46] Without his being aware of it, apparently, Perry's democratic prejudices betrayed him into elevating the commonplace and popular into standards of excellence. He disparages the achievement of Emily Dickinson, Poe, and even Hawthorne because they do not reflect the "typical qualities" of the American mind, and he overestimates the achievements of Longfellow and Whittier because they do reflect such qualities. He holds up popularity as a test for genuinely American literature— "books written for the great common audience of American men and women, like the novels of Winston Churchill" and the poems of James Whitcomb Riley and Sam Walter Foss, who wanted to "live in a house by the side of the road" and be a "friend of man."[47] For Perry, the writer par excellence of democratic America was Fenimore Cooper. Cooper, Perry said,

cared nothing and knew nothing about conscious literary art; his style is diffuse, his syntax the despair of school teachers, and many of his characters are bores. . . . Professional novelists like Balzac, professional critics like Sainte Beuve, stand amazed at Fenimore Cooper's skill and power. The true engineering and architectural lines are there. They were not plotted out before hand like George Eliot's . . . your *Last of the Mohicans* will be

[46] *Ibid.*, 245.
[47] *Ibid.*, 227–28, 237–38.

21

instinctively, inevitably right, while your *Daniel Deronda* will be industriously wrong.[48]

Whereas Bliss Perry's chief bias was a kind of democratic sentimentalism, Robert Morss Lovett's bias was somewhat socialistic. It was on the basis of *Boston*'s social propaganda, as Lovett admitted, that he voted to give this book of Upton Sinclair's a Pulitzer prize in 1929, just as eight years earlier he had denounced the award to Edith Wharton's *The Age of Innocence* because its author was out of touch with social realities.[49] In his book-length study of Edith Wharton, Lovett dismisses her as one of the "voices whispering the last enchantments of the Victorian age." She is, he says, unfamiliar with the social problems today, and her refined art is therefore received with impatience by a world which has "reverted toward barbarism," and which now sternly and realistically recognizes "the battle for survival" as the "cardinal fact in human biology."[50] Lovett's socialism, though somewhat less sentimental than Perry's democratic bias, was not always involved in his judgments of contemporary fiction. At least his standards were flexible enough to accommodate Booth Tarkington, Upton Sinclair, Sinclair Lewis, and Margaret Ayer Barnes.[51]

Stuart Pratt Sherman, who was younger than Perry and

[48] *A Study of Prose Fiction* (New York, 1902), 235–60. In this study, written primarily for college students, Perry places Hawthorne among the top three prose writers, the other two being Cooper and Poe. He felt that James and Twain did not quite measure up to their predecessors.

[49] Lovett, "Pulitzer Prize," *New Republic*, Vol. LX (Sept. 11, 1929), 100.

[50] *Edith Wharton* (New York, 1926), 86–87.

[51] Lovett rather lavishly praised *The Magnificent Ambersons* in a review in the *Dial* (*Book Review Digest*, 1918, p. 431). In *Preface to Fiction* (p. 83), he mentioned Margaret Ayer Barnes's Pulitzer prize winner, *Years of Grace*, as an American example of the genealogical novel. In his introduction to *Preface* (p. 10), he said that since the novel is "essentially popular," it "should demand of the layman no deeply specialized knowledge."

Lovett, was, in theory at least, more purely literary in his criticism. He ridiculed the moralistic attitude of several older jurors and disagreed with Lovett's final pronouncement against Mrs. Wharton.[52] In his essays he holds up as important fictional criteria both structure and style.[53] But like his colleagues Perry and Lovett, Sherman was deeply committed to the theory that fiction is a means of social uplift. He believed that America in the 1920's was uncivilized, remarkably vulgar, and self-satisfied, and that it was the function of the fiction writer to jolt the average man into an awareness of his plight and point the way toward cultural salvation. Sherman especially liked Sinclair Lewis' *Main Street* because he felt it had such a cathartic power, and for this quality he voted to give it a prize.[54]

Sherman's plan for cultural salvation is "service," not in the old-fashioned sense of missionary work in Africa or the Y.M.C.A., but work—"all work that is done as it should be done whether of the hands or of the brain." Such work, Sherman says, "whatever it is," has "something of the peace and satisfaction of religious devotion."[55] Sherman's theories about work and service are especially interesting because they resemble sentiments expressed in several Pulitzer prize novels.

[52] *Stuart P. Sherman*, II, 400, 402, and Sherman, *Main Stream*, 209–12.

[53] In commenting on the various candidates for the prize in 1922, Sherman said of *The Girls*, by Edna Ferber: "It has considerable breadth. Its style impressed me as undistinguished." Of *Erick Dorn*, by Floyd Dell, he said: "I have found it extraordinarily interesting in style and in the central series of characterizations. The most 'original' novel of the year, so far." Of *Three Soldiers*, by Dos Passos: "It has no great power in characterization or structure, but considerable interest as a commentary." (*Stuart P. Sherman*, II, 402–403.)

[54] Stuart P. Sherman, *The Significance of Sinclair Lewis* (New York, 1922). Essentially this was the same argument advanced by Robert Morss Lovett, "Pulitzer Prize," *New Republic*, Vol. XXVII (June 22, 1921), 114.

[55] *The Genius of America*, 171–95.

The body of his literary criticism, in fact, might serve as a gloss on *His Family*, *The Magnificent Ambersons*, *So Big*, and particularly *Alice Adams*, to which Sherman helped give a Pulitzer prize.

Finally, in addition to these eight men, we know of two professional fiction writers who served on Pulitzer novel juries: Hamlin Garland and Sinclair Lewis. One would expect these men to have been fairly astute judges of contemporary writing, or at least more sympathetic than their older and more theoretical colleagues. The fact is, however, they were not. At the time Garland served on the fiction jury he had become conservative in his literary judgments and somewhat bitter about his own lack of popular success. It seems possible that Garland helped keep *Main Street* from getting the Pulitzer prize in 1921 because he thought it an unfair and ignoble picture of small town life.[56]

Sinclair Lewis served on a fiction jury in 1936. He was then well out of the main stream of contemporary fiction; his preference continued to be for the by that time tedious debunking that he and H. L. Mencken had helped make so popular in the early 1920's. During the year Lewis served on a Pulitzer jury he voted to give the prize to H. L. Davis' *Honey in the Horn*, which, he said, was "one of those uncommon books that really express a land and an age and, by expressing them, really create them"—a remark that seems a garbled version of what Wilson Follet says about Lewis' own novel *Main Street*.[57] In choosing Davis' amateurish satire, Lewis and his colleagues passed by Steinbeck's *Tortilla Flat*, Faulkner's *Pylon*, Wolfe's *Of Time and the River*, and Ellen Glasgow's *Vein of Iron*.

[56] See Chap. II, p. 41 below.
[57] *New York Times*, May 5, 1936, p. 18; Wilson Follett, *The Modern Novel* (rev. ed., New York, 1923), *xxiii*.

Since 1936, when it was made known that Sinclair Lewis had served on the novel jury, the Pulitzer authorities have kept silent about their jurors and have also managed to keep their jurors from talking in public. And so, except for Dean Ackerman's general assurance in 1951 that the men who help select the Pulitzer prize-winning works are all members of respected American universities, the public has been given no information concerning who *really* is responsible for the Pulitzer prize decisions.[58] The general impression created by newspaper announcements is that the Pulitzer awards in both journalism and literature represent the judgment of the Advisory Board for (as it is now called) the Pulitzer Prizes.[59]

[58] Carl W. Ackerman, "Pulitzer Award Secrecy" (a letter to the editor), *Sat. Rev.*, Vol. XXXIV (July 14, 1951), 26.

[59] The novel juries whose members I have been able to establish are as follows: 1920: Stuart P. Sherman, Robert Grant, (third member unknown); 1921: Hamlin Garland, Stuart P. Sherman, Robert M. Lovett; 1922: Stuart P. Sherman, Samuel M. Crothers, Jefferson B. Fletcher; 1923: Jefferson B. Fletcher, Samuel M. Crothers, Bliss Perry; 1926: Richard Burton, Robert M. Lovett, Edwin Lefèvre; 1927: Richard Burton, Robert M. Lovett, Jefferson B. Fletcher; 1929: Richard Burton, Robert M. Lovett, Edwin Lefèvre; 1936: Sinclair Lewis (the other two members unknown).

CHAPTER TWO

The Establishment of the Tradition

WHEN THE FIRST Pulitzer prizes were awarded in 1917, the men who had brought the American novel so far in the last century—Mark Twain, Henry James, and Stephen Crane—were dead, and the giants of the new literary generation—F. Scott Fitzgerald, Ernest Hemingway, and William Faulkner—had not yet arisen to take their places.[1] But there were talented novelists on the literary scene: William Dean Howells, Edith Wharton, and Theodore Dreiser (who had not yet written *An American Tragedy*) were probably the most eminent. Of lesser-known young writers, there was Sherwood Anderson, who had brought out *Windy McPherson's Son* in 1916, just in time to be eligible for the first fiction prize, and also Willa Cather, Ellen Glasgow, and Gertrude Stein. Miss Cather had published *O Pioneers!* in 1913 and *The Song of the Lark* in 1915. Miss Glasgow had already produced a dozen books by 1917, and Gertrude Stein, having launched her career in experi-

[1] The history and biography prizes were inconspicuously awarded in 1917 at the end of commencement exercises at Columbia, and they received only brief mention in the newspapers. At the time, nothing was said about the failure to award the novel prize. The next year when the first novel award was given, the *New York Times* (June 3, 1918, p. 7), reported that no prize in fiction had been awarded last year because it was thought no novels had merited it.

mental writing with *Three Lives* in 1909, followed that with *Tender Buttons* in 1914.

But as it turned out, the year of 1917 was not especially productive of good novels. However, there were at least four respectable candidates for the first Pulitzer prize in fiction. A jury made up of even moderately perceptive literary experts might have recognized that Ellen Glasglow's *Life and Gabriella* was considerably better than average, or might have sensed behind Sherwood Anderson's *Windy McPherson's Son* a new talent worth encouraging. And certainly the two novels of William Dean Howells that were available (*The Leatherwood God* and *Daughter of the Storage*), though not especially significant, were both well written, prize-worthy books. Nevertheless, for reasons that only can be guessed at, the Pulitzer authorities did not give a novel prize in 1917. Perhaps the machinery for selecting the winning novel had not yet been set up; or, more probably, perhaps it appeared to the jurors that no novel published in 1916 was worthy of the prize. For though some of the drama jurors were to deny that they felt bound by the specifications laid down by Joseph Pulitzer, the novel jurors, from the beginning, consciously or unconsciously, were committed to a preference for a certain kind of moralistic fiction.

This at least is suggested by the fact that though there was again little to choose from the next year, the Pulitzer judges voted to give their first novel prize to a work that is only somewhat more sophisticated and just a little better written than the rags-to-riches romances of Horatio Alger. The first Pulitzer prize novel was *His Family*, by Ernest Poole, a former settlement worker, labor-union publicist and correspondent for *Outlook* and the *Saturday Evening Post*.[2]

[2] Stanley J. Kunitz and Howard Haycraft (eds.), *Twentieth Century Authors* (New York, 1942), 1,116.

Poole is best remembered today for an earlier novel, *The Harbor*, which, like *His Family*, is a crude imitation of the social history novels of H. G. Wells and John Galsworthy. In *The Harbor*, Poole depicts what he conceives to be the three periods of American economic growth: the reign of small competitive business; the then present world of corporation control; and the world of syndicalistic control that seemed to Poole to be hovering on the horizon in 1915.[3] Despite Poole's proletarian sympathies, the conclusion of this novel shows that he was not overtly advocating syndicalistic control. His hero takes a neutral position (the kind of position, by the way, that was to become fairly popular among Pulitzer novelists): He throws his lot in with history because, he says, the world is in a state of continual flux; different conditions demanded different loyalties and different values, and he will have to wait and see what tomorrow brings before committing himself to a course of action.

By the time he wrote *His Family*, Poole's loyalties had shifted from a belief in syndicalism to a kind of sentimental socialism; economic evolution is forgotten and we are back in a world of small competitive business wherein personal and social insolvency can be relieved by the practice of individualism and the correlated virtues of perseverance, thrift, sobriety, and devotion to work. Poole does not completely reject a belief in the obligations of society to promote the welfare of the indigent working class, but instead of syndicalism, he seems to favor "social service," a paternalistic humanitarianism.[4] In fact, *His Family* may be regarded as an

[3] Vernon Louis Parrington, *Main Currents in American Thought; An Interpretation of American Literature from the Beginnings to 1920*, III (New York, 1930), 349–50.

[4] It was exactly this point of view that Randolph Bourne took issue with in "This Older Generation," . . . *History of a Literary Radical, and Other Essays*, edited, with an introduction by Van Wyck Brooks (New York, 1920), 113, 117.

extended answer to the rhetorical question: How can one adjust to the conflicting claims of individualism and social responsibility? Roger Gale, the protagonist, and his three grown daughters appear almost allegorically to represent four possible answers.

The eldest daughter, standing for pre-industrial American values, lives only for her immediate family. She is a good mother, but lacks a sense of social responsibility. The middle daughter, being dedicated to her social work in the tenement district, has social awareness but neglects her family responsibilities. The youngest daughter lacks both the old familial virtues and social awareness. She is meant to represent new, war-time America: fast, selfish, and dedicated only to the pursuit of pleasure.

Poole's thesis is illustrated by Roger Gale, the father, a model of the right kind of person. Gale's career shows how individualism, social service, and familial virtue can be effectively balanced. Gale takes Johnny, a poor crippled boy, into his home and then into his business. Everything goes smoothly until the oldest daughter discovers that Johnny has tuberculosis; thinking only of herself and her family, she forces the poor boy out of her father's house. Johnny, however, remains in Gale's business (a newspaper-clipping service) and discovers a technique which puts it on a more solid financial basis. In a few years the boy is dead, but he leaves his half of the business to Gale, who then sells it and uses the money to pay off the mortgage he had assumed in order to take care of the very daughter who turned out the hard-working crippled boy.

Judged even by the standards of commercial fiction, *His Family* is not much of a novel. It is rather obvious propaganda designed for middle-class readers who wish to sympathize with the poor but who do not wish to see any changes in the economic *status quo*. By means of one limited and absurdly sentimental example, Poole attempts to show that the ideals of social service can be painlessly adapted to the traditional American belief in rugged individualism. And social service is recommended mainly on the grounds that it redounds to the economic interests of those who practice it. Although this may be an effective propaganda device, it can hardly be said to reflect a sophisticated moral appeal. The book is such an amateurish performance that there would be little point in discussing its artistic qualities if it might not be supposed by some readers who remember Poole's reputation as a serious novelist (*The Harbor* was both a popular and critical success) that his fictional talents are here being undervalued. One sample of his style and technique should suffice to scotch such speculations. In the following passage Poole describes Roger Gale as he makes his way through a slum district on his way to pawn a prized ring collection. This is a crucial point in Poole's story, since the slum experience is supposed to transform Gale from a selfish rich man to one sympathetic to the poor.

> Later he went for his evening walk. And as though drawn by invisible chains he strayed far down into the ghetto. Soon he was elbowing his way through a maze of uproarious tenement streets as one who has been there many times. But he noticed little around him. He went on, as he had always gone, seeing and hearing this seething life only as a background to his own adventures. He reached his destination. Pushing his way through a swarm of urchins playing in front of a pawn shop, he entered and was a long time inside, and when he came out again at last the whole expression of his face had undergone a striking change. As one who had found the solace he needed for the moment, his pace unconsciously quickened and he looked about him with brighter eyes.[5]

[5] *His Family* (New York, Macmillan Co., 1917), 41.

Poole's technique in this passage, as in the rest of the novel is that of the popular polemicist, concerned more with constructing characters and plot situations that illustrate his thesis than with creating fiction. He wants his readers to believe that the pawning of the ring collection (symbol!) alters Roger Gale's attitude toward the poor, but instead of dramatizing the situation and thus preparing him (and us) for Gale's change of heart, Poole merely hooks together a number of descriptive clichés. Instead of following Gale inside the pawn shop as his point of view commits him to doing, Poole posts himself outside, so that instead of having to make this extraordinary change convincing, he need only report those telltale changes in Gale's physiognomy—the "quickened step" and "brighter eyes"—in order to tell us the crisis is over and the tide has turned.

Social service and concern for the impoverished working classes was already somewhat passé as America approached the 1920's and the era of resurgent laissez faireism, big money, and "rugged individualism."[6] The next few Pulitzer prize decisions suggest that the fiction jurymen were sensitive to the changing currents of popular opinion. Ernest Poole had not gone so far, in *His Family*, as to suggest that a poor boy, even if crippled, should be assisted up the ladder of financial success if he could not climb part way by himself, but there is in Poole's novel a kind of sentimental regard for the poor that is not to be found in any of his immediate successors. The Pulitzer novels from 1919 on were to be less tolerant of those who, handicapped or not, were too weak to make their way unaided.

The first of these new novels to sentimentalize rugged individualism and denigrate the practitioners of spineless

[6] Merle Curti, *The Growth of American Thought* (2nd ed., New York, 1951), 692–704.

living is Booth Tarkington's *The Magnificent Ambersons* (1919). It is a somewhat better novel than *His Family*, but vastly inferior to Willa Cather's *My Antonia* which was also available for a Pulitzer prize in 1919. It is doubtful, however, that Willa Cather's novel was even seriously considered, for it was a balanced treatment of life on the Nebraska frontier and offered no easy moral lessons. Tarkington, on the contrary, was already a very popular writer, not only with the book-buying public that had taken *Penrod* to its heart in 1914, but with reviewers and critics, too. In fact, Tarkington's appeal was such that he won a second Pulitzer prize in 1922 for *Alice Adams*, a novel the fiction jurors thought of more literary merit than Dos Passos' *Three Soldiers*, which was also eligible for the prize that year.[7]

The Magnificent Ambersons is the story of George Minafer, a young man who thinks himself better than anyone else in town simply because he is an "aristocrat" (i.e., the third generation of the rich Amberson family). George dislikes Eugene Morgan, the father of his fiancée, because, though rich, Morgan is self-made. Tarkington shows how, as the fortune of the Ambersons declines, the fortunes of Eugene Morgan rise, until at the end of the book, Eugene is a great automotive industrialist and George is a nobody.

In *Alice Adams*, written three years after *The Magnificent Ambersons*, Tarkington treats the same problem from a different angle. Alice Adams is a poor girl who aspires to marry into a rich family. Like George (after his fall), Alice has nothing but intangibles to recommend her—manners, pretensions, personal desires; and, also like George, Alice is finally obliged by her author to kneel at the lowest rung of

[7] Of *Three Soldiers*, Stuart Pratt Sherman, chairman of the novel jury, wrote that it "has much current interest and has made its sensation as an attack on the A.E.F. It has no great power in characterization or structure but has considerable interest as a commentary." *Stuart P. Sherman*, II, 402.

the economic and social ladder. The difference between George's and Alice's fate is (and this may have led some critics to consider *Alice Adams* more realistic than *The Magnificent Ambersons*) that whereas George is reunited with his rich partner and restored to wealth, Alice loses hers and has to struggle on alone.

Although Tarkington may have been somewhat influenced by Henry James (as he maintained) and John Galsworthy—an influence that is clear enough—Tarkington's ideas and techniques are much simpler than either James' or Galsworthy's.[8] There is one simple idea behind both of Tarkington's prize-winning novels which provides not only the theme of each work but which is also the guiding principle in the creation of characters and the construction of plot: honest work will be rewarded by success.

In both novels, the ethical center is occupied by characters who illustrate this truth and are embodiments of the appropriate virtues and successes. *The Magnificent Ambersons* has two such characters, Major Amberson, founder of the Amberson fortune, and his spiritual heir, Eugene Morgan. Major Amberson had applied the doctrine of individualism in the days when money could be made by land speculation; Eugene Morgan applies it under the new conditions imposed by the automobile. Major Amberson and Eugene Morgan are set up as the norms for assessing the progressive degeneration of the Amberson line. The son, George Amberson, who was only slightly snobbish, managed to hold down a government job for a time, but the grandson, George Minafer, refuses absolutely to do any kind of work. Lucy Morgan is shocked at George's attitude and refuses to become engaged to him because she knows her father will not

[8] James Leslie Woodress, *Booth Tarkington, Gentleman from Indiana* (Philadelphia, 1955), 247.

33

approve of such an idle young man. The career of Eugene, mirroring the career of Major Amberson, shows that rugged individualism is still possible in 1918, though under altered conditions, and that personally acquired, rather than inherited wealth, is indispensable for developing the right kind of character.

It is the fate of George that drives home the moral. After George's grandfather dies, it is discovered that the Amberson fortune has dwindled to nothing, and George has been left penniless. Moreover, the automobile to which Eugene Morgan's fortune is linked has transformed the little town into a city where George Minafer can no longer be recognized and looked up to. He is obliged to take a job as a laborer in order to support himself and his maiden aunt, and, of course, the job turns out to be the making of him. He accepts industrial progress even though it has knocked him down (literally, in fact, in the form of a motor truck). After the proper amount of travail, George is redeemed, released from the drudgery of his job, and given the hand of the beautiful rich girl. Democratic now, he even asks Eugene's forgiveness for his past snobbishness. The implication is that he will find his place high in Morgan's automobile factory.

Between 1918 and 1921, alterations in American life brought on by war-time upheavals and boom time prosperity began to make themselves generally felt. Not only were the sons and daughters of the rich seeking to live in idleness, it seems, but the offspring of the working classes were also hankering after a life of ease and elegance. Public moralists were much concerned about this new dissatisfaction and pleasure-seeking. Stuart Pratt Sherman said that work, any kind of work, "whether of the hand or of the brain," was the only satisfactory road to happiness.[9] And Booth Tarkington's

[9] *The Genius of America,* 171.

34

second Pulitzer prize-winning novel (which Sherman helped select) is a homily on that theme.[10] *Alice Adams* is the story of a poor family, the members of which lie, cheat, steal, and try to marry their way into wealth and social prominence.

At the ethical center of *Alice Adams* is old Mr. Lamb, who founded Lamb & Company:

> Probably the last great merchant in America to wear the chin beard . . . . Files of old magazines of that period might show him in woodcut, as, "Type of Boston Merchant." Nast might have drawn him as an honest statesman. He was eighty, hale and sturdy, not aged; and his quick blue eyes, still unflecked and as brisk as a boy's, saw everything.[11]

Alice's father, Virgil, is Lamb's opposite: an old man at fifty, sick, broken in spirit, an absolute liability at his job in Mr. Lamb's mercantile house. Instead of "taking some pride" in the noises of the city as proof of "his citizenship in a live town," he "merely hated them because they kept him awake. They 'pressed his nerves' as he put it; and so did almost everything else, for that matter."[12] Mr. Lamb gives Virgil a job, keeps him on when he becomes sick and no longer of use to the firm, visits him at home. Later, after Virgil has set himself up in the glue-making business and is in financial difficulties, Mr. Lamb buys out the business (even though Adams had stolen the glue formula from him), helps pay off the mortgage on the Adams's house, and keeps the Adams's son from going to jail. But Mr. Lamb is no Pollyanna. Before coming to Virgil's rescue, he goes to great lengths to teach Virgil a lesson about business morality. He opens a big glue-works across the street from Adams's little

---

[10] *Stuart P. Sherman*, II, 402–403.
[11] Tarkington, *Alice Adams* (Garden City, N.Y., Doubleday, Page & Co., 1921), 178. (All quotations are from this edition.)
[12] *Ibid.*, 6.

make-shift plant, and quickly brings Adams to his knees. When Adams comes over one day, Mr. Lamb lectures him as follows:

> I got just one right important thing to tell you before we talk any further business, and that's this: there's some few men in this town made their money in off-color ways, but there aren't many; and those there are have had to be a darn sight slicker than you know how to be, or ever *will* know how to be. Yes, sir, and they none of them had the little gumption to try to make it out of a man that had the spirit not to let 'em![13]

Mr. Lamb is a man much sinned against by the Adamses. Walter Adams, Virgil's good-for-nothing son (he drinks and gambles) absconds with three hundred and fifty dollars of Lamb and Company's funds. Walter's crime precipitates the breakdown of his father's health and hastens the failure of his glue business—a chain of cause and effect which only goes to show that people get exactly what they deserve in this world, or as one character in *The Magnificent Ambersons* puts it, "I never saw a plainer case of a person's fault making them pay for having it."[14] Mr. Lamb's generous purchase of the Adams' glue-works includes enough money to cover Walter's theft and to pay off the mortgage, too.

Mr. Adams' and Walter's thievery is more obviously criminal than the crime of the book's central character, Alice Adams. Her crime—or sin as it had better be called—is committed against the sacred precept that a life of toil is the poor man's (or woman's) allotted happiness. Alice has romantic dreams of moving in fashionable society and marrying a rich young man. Her empty-headed mother encourages her, and helps her get the necessary party dresses which her father's

---

[13] *Ibid.*, 402–403.
[14] Tarkington, *The Magnificent Ambersons* (Garden City, New York, Doubleday, Page, & Co., 1919), 382. (All quotations are from this edition.)

wages cannot provide. The girl manages to attract the attention of a rich young man, but just as she seems on the point of securing him, the gossip about her father's appropriation of the glue formula causes him to defect.

But salvation, through purgation, is possible for a sinner. Alice starts out on a mysterious pilgrimage with the advice and blessings of her father, Virgil, who by this time has learned his lesson and is now a fit, if exhausted guide. Her first encounter is with her former suitor whom she has not seen since the night he defected. She meets him on this last occasion with a smile, cordial but brisk, and passes on, taking "some pride in herself for the way she had met this little crisis." But no sooner has she got within sight of that "portal of doom" (Frincke's Business College) than there is temptation: her "old habit of dramatizing herself still prevails with her."

> There came into her mind a whimsical comparison of her fate with that of the heroine in a French romance . . . . The story ended with the heroine's taking the veil after a death blow to love; and the final scene again became vivid to Alice, for a moment. . . . she seemed herself to stand among the great shadows in the cathedral nave; smelled the smoky incense on the enclosed air, heard the solemn peal of the organ. She remembered how the novice's father knelt, trembling, beside a pillar of gray stone; how the faithless lover watched and shivered behind the statue of a saint . . . .[15]

Having established his symbolic reference—the romantic mysticism of dream—Tarkington has Alice fight down the temptation with an appeal to the *mystique* of the practical:

> It was the vision of a moment only, and for no longer than a moment did Alice tell herself that the romance provided a

[15] All quotations relating to this scene are from *Alice Adams*, 431–34.

37

prettier way of taking the veil than she had chosen, and that a faithless lover, shaking with remorse behind a saint's statue, was a greater solace than one left on a street corner protesting that he'd like to call sometime—if he could.

Then Alice arrives at the portal of her purgatory:

> . . . that dark entrance to the wooden stairway leading up to Frincke's Business College—the very doorway she had always looked upon as the end of youth and the end of hope. How often she had thought of this obscurity as something lying in wait to obliterate the footsteps of any girl who should ascend into the smoky darkness above.

Though Alice does not take the veil of the French romance, she does join the sisterhood of business women—"old maids of a dozen different types, yet all looking a little like herself." But instead of the horrors Alice had imagined, her pilgrimage, like Dante's ascent of the mountain of purgatory, leads into the sunlight of the empyrean:

> Half-way up the shadows were heaviest, but after that the place began to seem brighter. There was an open window overhead somewhere, she found, and the steps at the top were gay with sunshine.

Spoiled-girl Alice, like spoiled-boy George, sees the light and feels its joy. She will, somehow, work her way to forgiveness and success. Both of Tarkington's novels beautifully illustrate the truth of Fitzgerald's remark in the opening section of "The Rich Boy," that if you begin with a type, you end up with a stereotype. When Tarkington wrote *The Magnificent Ambersons,* his conception of a rich snob was the popular notion of somebody expensively dressed, walking about with his nose in the air. When Tarkington wishes to invoke George's snobbism, he brings him onto the stage, has him display his fine clothes and haughty demeanor, and then

depart. Sometimes in an unusual display of rampant snobbism, George even shouts out loud several times the "hard
term" he had "employed since childhood's scornful hour"—
"Riffraff!"[16] Mr. and Mrs. Adams are also straight out of
popular cliché; he is the hen-pecked husband, long-suffering,
spineless; she is the scold and social climber. And so it goes
with Mr. Lamb, Alice, and all the rest.

In 1920, the year after the award to Booth Tarkington
for *The Magnificent Ambersons*, the Pulitzer authorities
gave no prize in fiction even though Sherwood Anderson's
Winesburg, Ohio was eligible. Had this unusual and not
completely "wholesome" volume been proposed by any of
the jurors, it would understandably have run into stiff opposition from the older, more conservative members of the
jury. But it is more difficult to see why Ellen Glasgow's *The
Builders* was also passed over. Judging from the kind of book
usually preferred, perhaps its treatment of Southern material
was not thought sufficiently "American," and perhaps Miss
Glasgow's style was adjudged as too subtle to "sustain
interest."

In 1921, between the two awards to Booth Tarkington,
the Pulitzer authorities made what was to be one of their
best decisions, although there is evidence that this was an
accident of circumstances. In 1921 the prize was given to *The
Age of Innocence*, by Edith Wharton. In contrast to Poole's
and Tarkington's popular melodramas, *The Age of Innocence* is a quiet, mildly ironic novel of manners. Much indebted to Henry James, this almost first-rate novel is
intelligently and competently written. Instead of holding up
stereotyped Europeans, corrupt and immoral, as a foil to

[16] *Alice Adams*, 270.

American goodness and wholesomeness (as some later Pulitzer novels were to do), Mrs. Wharton's book dramatically
contrasts a sophisticated, Europeanized American with
straight-laced, shallow New York society people of the 1870's,
a period which some of the Pulitzer jurors might have been
expected to regard as "finely" and "beautifully" American.[17]
On the other hand, since Mrs. Wharton in her polite way is
bitingly critical of conventional black-and-white morality,
one might well wonder why her novel happened to be given
a Pulitzer prize.

The answer appears to be that *The Age of Innocence*
was chosen not so much because of what it was, but because
of what it was not. The Advisory Board (or whoever made
the final decision) was put in the position of having to choose
between Mrs. Wharton's satire of 1870's upper-class New
York society and Sinclair Lewis' satire of 1920's small-town
middle western society. Clearly, *Main Street* was the more
controversial book. It was widely read, hotly discussed, and
commonly regarded as a vicious attack on small-town culture,
or lack of culture. *The Age of Innocence*, though deeply critical, was urbane, good mannered, and uncontroversial. One
could read it without being aware that it dealt with anything
more than the quaint past, for its attack on American life
was not open and palpable.

Although Lewis' novel shocked and outraged many

17 Hamlin Garland noted in his diary in 1920, the year *The Age of
Innocence* was published, that the old life of New York was passing away
along with the old Nordic race that used to inhabit it, "the tall, grey eyed,
straight-nosed aristocrats of other years." Literature today, he said, is too full
of libertinism and sex, and American novelists are imitating the worst aspects
of Europe—*My Friendly Contemporaries* (New York, 1932), 347. Robert
Grant—*Fourscore, An Autobiography* (New York, 1934), 102–23, 236—
felt that the older Eastern society was considerably superior to the classless
Middle West, as his book, *Unleavened Bread*, indicated; he liked *Main
Street* because Lewis ridiculed Middle Western boorishness.

readers, it was hailed enthusiastically both here and in England by writers and literary critics. Among those who sent Lewis letters of praise were John Galsworthy and Hamlin Garland, whose own books about the bleakness of life in the Middle West had figured in the ancestry of *Main Street* and who, as it turned out, served as chairman of the novel jury the year *Main Street* was eligible for the Pulitzer prize. However, sometime between his letter to Lewis and the casting of his ballot in 1921, Garland, it seems, changed his mind about *Main Street*. At least, he recorded in his diary this same year a remark which would hardly seem to suggest that he intended to recommend it for the Pulitzer novel prize.[18] I found *Main Street*, he wrote, very "depressing, . . . vicious, and vengeful," and he concluded that Lewis was merely "taking it out of [*sic*] the small Middle Western town."[19] Whether Garland kept *Main Street* from getting the prize or whether President Butler vetoed the decision is not public knowledge.[20] It is known, however, that the two other novel jurymen in 1921, Stuart Pratt Sherman and Robert Morss Lovett, had both given *Main Street* first place on their ballots and fully expected that it would be declared the winner. When *The Age of Innocence* was handed the prize instead,

[18] Mark Schorer, *Sinclair Lewis* (New York, 1961), 274.
[19] *My Friendly Contemporaries*, 337–38.
[20] At the time Lovett wrote his account for *New Republic* (June 22, 1921), he believed the committee was unanimous in voting for *Main Street* and that the Columbia authorities and the Advisory Board were responsible for the overruling. That was also the impression of Sinclair Lewis and it is still apparently held by Lewis' publisher and by his biographer. (See Schorer, *Sinclair Lewis*, 269). But Stuart Pratt Sherman was advised by F. D. Fackenthal, secretary of Columbia, that in giving the award to *The Age of Innocence*, the Advisory Board was not at fault. (See *Stuart P. Sherman*, II, 401–402.) Sherman was sufficiently satisfied with this explanation to serve on the committee next year. The fact that Garland disliked *Main Street* and that, as chairman, he was to transmit the jury's decision to the Columbia officials, suggests rather strongly that Garland may have been responsible for keeping *Main Street* from getting the award.

they were both incensed. Sherman threatened not to serve on the juries again, and Lovett vented his ire against the Pulitzer authorities by abandoning the anonymity usually kept by Pulitzer jurors and by criticizing the decision openly in a letter to the *New Republic*.[21] He also gave his and Sherman's reason for preferring *Main Street* over *The Age of Innocence*. Mrs. Wharton's novel, he said, was dead, whereas Lewis' was a living commentary on the American scene. Moreover, he felt, *The Age of Innocence* did not fulfill the conditions of the donor's will, whereas *Main Street*, "through its social criticism, had led its readers to purge the small-town atmosphere of certain unwholesome tendencies . . . . It set up an effective standard and actually accomplished something toward its attainment."[22]

Judged apart from the circumstances which brought it an award, *The Age of Innocence* was a better choice than *Main Street*. Not only is Mrs. Wharton's craftsmanship superior to Lewis', but with the passing of time and the dissipation of *Main Street*'s social relevance, Mrs. Wharton's novel stands out as a much deeper and more significant criticism of American manners. In terms of the history of the Pulitzer prize, however, the victory of *The Age of Innocence* over *Main Street* must be set down as a triumph of the innocuous—as a preference for the old American tradition, as Garland might have said, as against the new, vulgar, vengeful "literature of revolt" derived from the Germanic barbarism of H. L. Mencken and the cruel satire of Flaubert.

After *Main Street*'s failure to take the prize even when the jury was dominated by the young "liberals," it was hardly likely that *Babbitt* was given very serious consideration in

[21] *Stuart P. Sherman*, II, 401.
[22] Robert Morss Lovett, "Pulitzer Prize," *New Republic*, Vol. XXVII (June 22, 1921), 114; and *Stuart P. Sherman*, II, 401.

1923; for in that year the old guard was in full control of the jury and had a very strong contender in one of Willa Cather's weaker novels, *One of Ours,* the story of a young man's sacrifice in the Great War.[23] The hero of Miss Cather's novel, Claude Wheeler, was born and reared on a farm in the Middle West. Like Carol Kennicott of *Main Street,* Claude yearns to improve himself culturally, but his parents cannot understand his taste for refinements and they prevent his attending the university and dedicating himself to the academic pursuit of culture. He is a faithful son and attempts to shape his ambitions to their limited vision, but because of an accident which puts him to bed for a long time, he falls in love with his nurse, Enid Royce, a peculiar young woman, whose mother and sister are religious fanatics. Claude persuades Enid to marry him and intends to follow the normal, workaday life which his family wants him to live, but Enid turns out to be sexually frigid. She repulses Claude and flees to China to work in the missions. Dejection follows his latest failure to adapt himself to the normal, but Claude lifts himself from the prison of his purposeless existence, joins the United States Army and embarks on the cause of saving civilization from the Hun. Claude becomes an officer, goes overseas and falls in love with France and her beautiful culture. At last he finds a cause worthy of his complete dedication. One day at the front, he stands up and deliberately leads his platoon into the German guns.

Several reviewers argued the success or failure of Miss Cather's novel along the lines of whether or not war was the noble cause which she and her hero considered it.[24] Robert Morss Lovett praised the book for its patriotic sentiments,

[23] Novel jurors in 1923: Jefferson B. Fletcher, chairman; Samuel M. Crothers, and Bliss Perry.

[24] *Book Review Digest* (1922), pp. 95–96.

while Heywood Broun damned it, asserting that war was too high a price to pay even for the saving of a human soul. *One of Ours* fails artistically, however, as some of the critics in the journals pointed out, mainly because Miss Cather is unable to create convincingly her hero's experience. The second half of the book, which deals with Claude's experiences in the army, is convincingly detailed (the author researched her facts), but there are some serious discrepancies between what Willa Cather asserts about her hero's feelings and what she manages to create. The conclusion of the novel comes off, in other words, only if one is prepared to believe, as Miss Cather there does, that World War I is a noble cause.

The first part of *One of Ours* is more believable than the last, but it too suffers from some of the same deficiencies. As Edmund Wilson has pointed out, Miss Cather's characters are little more than cardboard figures which she manipulates mechanically according to plan.[25] Terrible things happen to the outside of her characters, but in spite of this, nothing seems to happen to them inside. In fact, Miss Cather's materials keep pointing her toward conclusions quite different from those she was willing to draw about the suffering of her characters and the inadequacy of their solutions. Claude Wheeler finds farm life in the Middle West an intolerable, sterile existence. And, a thing the Pulitzer judges did not take into account—the fact that Claude and his wife are obliged to leave their homes and find things to live for in alien lands—seems a deeper and more damaging criticism of American life than that found either in *Main Street* or *Babbitt*.

One of Ours differs from earlier Pulitzer novels in the largeness of its idealism. Whereas Poole and Tarkington hold

[25] *The Shores of Light: A Literary Chronicle of the Twenties* (New York, 1952), 40.

44

their heroes and heroines up to the ethics of the cashbox, Miss Cather holds hers up to the nobler, if somewhat more shadowy, ideals of "culture" and "civilization." In spite of this difference and the fact that it is more sensitively written than Pulitzer prize books usually are, *One of Ours* is similar in one important way to a number of other prize winners. Its "happy" ending (like that of *Alice Adams* and, many years later, of Herman Wouk's *The Caine Mutiny*) depends upon bending the rebellious individual to the collective will. Claude Wheeler leads his troops into the fire of German guns. For "individualism" in Pulitzer prize fiction means merely the liberty to succeed in ways popularly subscribed to in American society, not the right to be oneself.

Considering, in 1923, the newness of the Pulitzer awards and the fact that a number of men with somewhat different tastes and standards served on these juries, it would not be surprising to find an absence of direction in these early decisions. Indeed, if one considers only the titles of the prize works and the reputations of the authors, it would seem that the charge Sinclair Lewis was soon to make, that the Pulitzer novel tradition merely reflects the taste of a haphazard committee, is indeed correct and that the Pulitzer roster is nothing more than a random collection of unrelated books.[26] Although there is some truth in Lewis' charge (certainly *The Age of Innocence* and perhaps even *One of Ours* is out of place here), a larger truth is that there is discernible even in these early decisions a definite pattern of preference, a preference for novels that have to do chiefly with the theme of economic individualism and with the belief that virtue consists of making money by the sweat of one's brow. Looking further ahead, one can also see that this theme was to be popular not only during the first decade of the prize's history,

[26] See Chap. III below.

but on and off for something like the next forty years. One might indeed say that this belief, that virtue inheres in economic individualism, constitutes the one principal theme of the Pulitzer novel prize tradition.

CHAPTER THREE

Consolidation of the Tradition

APOLOGISTS for the Pulitzer awards have pointed out what a disadvantage it is that the prize must be given for a book published during one calendar year, for in some years there may be several good novels available, while in others there may be none. This inequality in the distribution of good fiction, it is thought, probably accounts for the Pulitzer authorities' having passed over some deserving books.[1] Although it may be that the novels of some significant writers occasionally failed to receive prizes because they appeared during years when stronger candidates were available, that was not true of Sherwood Anderson's fiction in these early years. Anderson had been eligible in 1917 with *Windy McPherson's Son*, and again in 1920 with *Winesburg, Ohio*—years when the authorities declined to give an award. In 1924, Anderson was again eligible with *Many Marriages*, not a very good book to be sure, but no worse artistically than the derivative first novel that took the prize this year, *The Able McLaughlins*, by Margaret Wilson. Although Miss Wilson's talent cannot be called distinguished or original, there is this to be said in her favor: Her

[1] These are arguments I have heard in discussion. See also Carlos Baker, "Forty Years of Pulitzer Prizes," *Princeton Univ. Lib. Chron.*, Vol. XVIII (Winter, 1957), 42–45.

47

models were not the social histories of H. G. Wells and John Galsworthy. She drew instead on the native tradition of local color and the fictional tragedies of Thomas Hardy. The best qualities of *The Able McLaughlins* are its "facts"—the furniture of pioneer life: descriptions of simple meals, devout prayers, building of houses, the cozy hearth, the poor condition of roads, the hard life of women, and the stubbornness of men. Despite the presence of much convincing detail (an unusual quality in Pulitzer fiction), when it is judged as a novel, *The Able McLaughlins* is an amateurish performance. It lacks unity: the book consists of passages of realism for the sake of realism, a contrived love triangle (which is sentimentally resolved), and a Mary E. Wilkins Freeman-like episode (cf.'s "The Revolt of Mother") about a Scotch woman who tricks her husband into building a house. None of these elements in *The Able McLaughlins* are sufficiently related to justify being brought together in the same story.

There may have been extra-literary reasons for the selection of Miss Wilson's book, for its implicit interpretation of America's past fits neatly into the emerging pattern of Pulitzer novels about American life: simple people plus hard work (pioneer hardship) equals a "noble, inspiring picture" of America's past, a formula which Hamlin Garland, for one, would certainly have approved. *The Able McLaughlins* is, as we shall see, the first in a long series of Pulitzer books about the American frontier which agreeably combine sentimental "romance" under a glossy patina of realism.

In 1925, the Pulitzer authorities selected another very popular work of sentimental realism, *So Big*, by Edna Ferber. It was not by default, however, that Miss Ferber's took the prize this year. There is evidence to indicate that *So Big* was considered by some Pulitzer judges to be as good as, perhaps better than *The Age of Innocence.* At least, that seems to be the judgment of William Lyon Phelps, an officer of the American Academy, and for many years a member of the Pulitzer drama jury. Phelps said that *So Big* had given Miss Ferber "an international reputation" and "established her position in contemporary fiction." In its characters and in its setting, he said, *So Big*

> . . . is purely American . . . . It represents the triumph of a woman who found the hard, grinding toil of daily existence a thrilling romantic adventure; and yet it is wholly free from the shallow forced-draught cheerfulness which has wrecked so many American novels. The reason for this is twofold: Edna Ferber is a capable literary artist who distinguishes the genuine from the shoddy, and she knows what she is talking about. Her novels are built on experience.[2]

So Big is the story of Selina Peake DeJong, who is left penniless when her gambler father dies of a bullet wound. Even though she is still a young lady in finishing school, Selina has pluck and good common sense. She hates to leave her friend, Julie Hemple, and the little luxuries her father's erratic income occasionally provides, but Selina packs her trunk and goes to teach school at High Prairie, a little Dutch community outside Chicago. There she meets and marries Pervus DeJong and there, too, she finds shy Roelf Pool. She nurtures his love of beauty and sends him out into the world to become a great commercial artist. The union of Selina and Pervus is blessed with a son, Dirk ("So Big"), but it is cursed by Pervus' inefficiency and by his Dutch stubbornness. The inefficiency causes their farm to deteriorate and the

---

[2] *Twentieth Century American Novels* (Chicago, 1927), 17. Cf. Fred Lewis Pattee, *The New American Literature, 1890–1930* (New York, 1930), 323. Except for Edward Wagenknecht's *Cavalcade of the American Novel* (New York, 1952), recent books on American fiction fail to mention Edna Ferber.

stubbornness results in Pervus' early death. Selina is again left penniless, this time with a run-down farm, a young son to rear, and a battle to be fought with the deep prejudices of High Prairie against a mere woman's presuming to storm life's battlements alone. Undaunted, Selina pulls on her late husband's old clodhoppers and his felt hat and goes out into the field where, Miss Ferber tells us, "she literally tore a living out of the earth with her bare hands."

The DeJong farm prospers; Selina's son grows to young manhood, and she expects great things from him. She wants him to *do* something, something for the good of mankind, even as she is doing, and, as she has inspired Roelf Pool to do, something creative. But Dirk is soft and spoiled by Selina's money (she prospers in widowhood), and he wants only to indulge his taste for fancy clothes and fast living. He takes a job in the bond department of a bank—to the eternal disappointment of his mother. Her failure with her son is Selina's only defeat; but, as Miss Ferber tells us in her autobiography, *So Big* is the story of a defeat that is also a victory.[3] Selina's defeat with Dirk is counterbalanced by her victory with Roelf Pool, who returns in triumph to Chicago at the age of forty-five as an internationally famous portrait painter, accompanied by a famous French general. These celebrities are wined and dined by the best of Chicago society, but they manage to escape to the rustic simplicity of Selina's "beautiful quiet old farm." In the meantime, Dallas O'Mara, a young woman shortly to become a famous portrait painter in her own right, tells Dirk that his mother is a truly beautiful woman, "really distinguished looking—distinguishedly American." Dirk smiles as though at a joke, but Roelf, the famous portrait painter, agrees, paying Selina lavish compliments. There are, he says, only two kinds of people in the

[3] *A Peculiar Treasure* (New York, 1940), 277–81.

world who really matter—those who are "wheat" and those who are "emeralds." "You're wheat," Roelf tells Selina. And Selina graciously responds, "And you're emerald." While this lavish praise is being paid to his unstylish old mother, Dirk DeJong writhes in an agony of insufficiency while "something" inside him keeps saying, "You're nothing but a rubber stamp, Dirk DeJong. You're nothing but a rubber stamp, over and over."[4]

It does not require a very thoughtful reading of *So Big* to discover that Selina's victory is another extended homily on the gospel of rugged individualism. The facts of Selina's life are arranged to put her on her own: first, her father's death forces her to earn a living, and then her husband's death not only throws her back upon her own resources, but gives her a free hand to carry out the revolutionary plans she has for making Pervus' run-down farm a paying proposition. As in Tarkington's *The Magnificent Ambersons*, inherited wealth is shown to be a corrupting force because it prevents a man from lifting himself by his own bootstraps. This is one of the lessons which Selina and her failure with her son teach, and to underscore it, there is the counterbalancing example of Roelf Pool. Selina herself supplies the text: "You've seen the world, and you've got it in your hand. Little Roelf Pool. *And you did it all alone.* In spite of everything."[5]

To leave no doubt about the larger social and economic implications of her message, Miss Ferber introduces the character of August Hempel, a self-made Chicago millionaire packing house owner. As well as lending some money to Selina when she wishes to get her asparagus plantation started, August Hempel serves as the moral center of the

[4] Ferber, *So Big* (Garden City, New York, Doubleday, Page, & Co., 1924), 357–58. (All quotations are from this edition.)
[5] *Ibid.*, 356.

51

book, the standard by which the actions of the other characters may be measured. He is Miss Ferber's symbol of the great American type whose heirs are Selina and Roelf, the rags-to-riches heroes and heroines who "did it all alone, in spite of everything."

> August Hempel was to establish the famous Hempel Packing Company. At fifty he was the power in the yards, and there were Hempel branches in Kansas City, Omaha, Denver. At sixty you saw the name of Hempel plastered over packing sheds, factories, and canning plants all the way from Honolulu to Portland . . . . A magnificent old pirate sailing the perilous commercial seas of the American 90's before commissions, investigations, and inquisitive senate insisted on applying whitewash to the black flag of trade . . . .
>
> The Hempel Packing Company was a vast monster now stretching great arms into Europe, into South America. In some of the yellow journals that had cropped up in the last few years you saw old Aug himself portrayed in the cartoons as an octopus with cold slimy eyes and a hundred writhing reaching tentacles. These bothered Aug a little though he pretended to laugh at them. "What do they want to go to work and make me out like that for? I sell good meat for all I can get for it. That's business, ain't it?"[6]

The sentimental tale of Selina Peake DeJong is, of course, Edna Ferber's own way of applying whitewash to the black flag of trade. Selina, the asparagus queen, is another Hempel (Rockefeller, or Carnegie) in petticoats. She drags herself up out of the poverty-stricken fields into ownership of a big truck farming business and puts DeJong asparagus on the menus of all the finest restaurants in Chicago. Selina is the kind of woman Alice Adams, ideally, ought to have been. *Alice Adams*, however, is written from an upper middle-class

[6] *Ibid.*, 21, 218.

point of view, *So Big* from the angle of a lower middle class. Instead of the snobbery of house, furniture, and clothes by which Tarkington makes Alice's pretensions absurd, Miss Ferber shows that the poverty, shabbiness, and unstylishness of Selina make her much better than the Chicago snobs whose grandfathers a few years back were not a whit better than she. Selina's goodness is manifest by the fact that she wears an old coat-sweater and a battered hat, in contrast to her son's Roger Peel ("the English tailor") clothes. She prefers "lusterwear" and "Early American" and he goes in for heavy imitations of European "periods." She likes to walk; he likes to ride. She prefers the farm and the slums of Chicago, he prefers fashionable apartments.

Miss Ferber has denied that she writes her novels according to formula, as some of her critics have charged, and although it is admittedly difficult to imagine her writing *So Big* with an eye anywhere but on the market place, there is doubtless much truth in what she says.[7] For, if nothing else in the novel comes through very convincingly, Edna Ferber's admiration for Selina does. She loves and admires her heroine and the ideas she stands for. She obviously delights in putting Selina through her paces, jumping her over the barricades of class and sex, and having her arrive at the citadels of money and power flushed with victory. We feel Miss Ferber's triumph in having Selina spurn the symbols of wealth while the great men of two continents sit adoringly at her feet. It is of such stuff that daydreams are made.[8]

In *A Peculiar Treasure*, Miss Ferber records, rather

[7] *A Peculiar Treasure*, p. 281.

[8] Edna Ferber is recently reported to have said that since men have made a failure of running the world, "perhaps the women ought to use their powers, begin running things. They bear the children, rear them, keep the household budget. They may get us out of the woods yet." Nanette Kutner, "Edna Ferber Today," *Everywoman's Family Circle*, Vol. LXI (Feb., 1959), 51.

smugly, that contrary to what some people thought, at the time she wrote *So Big* she had never been on a farm.[9] That interesting information only confirms what must be apparent to anyone who reads *So Big* and does not fall under the spell of Miss Ferber's romance. For no rational person, whether or not he has grown up on a farm, could believe that a life devoted to "literally tearing a living out of the earth" could be such a "thrilling romantic adventure." Only someone with a fierce desire to believe in the possibility of Selina DeJong, and with a deep ignorance of the actualities from which she is supposed to spring, could have written such a book. Contrary to Professor Phelps's claims for her art, Miss Ferber's fierce tone of conviction is unmatched by either the logic of what she insists is the truth about Selina's experience, or by those experiences as Miss Ferber creates them. What happens inside Selina while the heroic struggle goes on? How does she feel as she stoops in the field day after day? These are questions which must be answered if the beautiful life of Selina can be taken as anything more than wish fulfillment. Indeed Miss Ferber's success depends upon *not* answering them, for the underlying appeal of *So Big* is the vigorous assertion that what cannot be, *is* true.

Miss Ferber's success also depends upon her ability to induce her audience to share her daydreams by reminding them of what they already "know"—from popular myths, sentimental fiction, comic strips, and movies. She appeals to the same myth exploited by Poole and Tarkington, that any American can, and *ought* to raise himself from rags to riches; and she appeals to another popular belief, that the best, most wholesome life for an American is on a farm. Her peculiar achievement is to take these myths, which at some points are contradictory, and wrap them up into one package and to

[9] Page 277.

reassert their primacy and their goodness. Selina, the perfect embodiment of the early Pulitzer code, is a symbol for all the abstractions which certain minds can uncritically accept as "good." She is an American mother, relatively uneducated but intelligent, a shrewd business woman, but also a kind-hearted neighbor. She is rich, but lives as though she is poor; she is a farm woman, but likes the city slums. She is practical but also artistic. The world is ugly, but she finds it beautiful. Though a small, thin woman, she is able to best the men in her family, to teach them, to outwork them, to outsmart them, to support them and, in the end, to have them sit at her feet and adore her. At one point, Miss Ferber likens Selina to the Virgin Mary.

Edna Ferber's brand of realism is the kind made familiar by the movies. She flashes a "shot" of Selina in the fields with her skirt tucked up and a man's hat jammed back on her head; or she shows Selina driving to market in an old farm wagon, with her son Dirk beside her and the vegetables piled up behind; or Selina may be seen condescending to have coffee with her neighbors, dispensing good advice with her cream and sugar. There are a few details sketched in—those familiar details which anyone who has read sentimental stories or been to the movies will recognize as "true to life."[10] On occasion, Miss Ferber does attempt the difficult task of creating Selina's experience, and it is from an examination of such attempts that we can most readily spot the wide gaps between what Miss Ferber asserts and what she actually manages to create.

Early in the book, when Miss Ferber is arranging matters so that Selina will be cast out on her own, she is obliged

[10] See especially passages on page 164 (that begin "If, then, you had been traveling the Halsted road . . .") and on page 354 (that begin "Then they saw her coming, a small dark figure against the back drop of sun and sky and fields . . .").

to get rid of Simeon Peake, Selina's father. Miss Ferber sets the stage in the boardinghouse to which Simeon's reverses of fortune have brought them. Selina is discovered alone, sewing a rose on her hat and waiting for her father's return. Suddenly, "she heard a sound. She had never heard that sound before —that peculiar sound—the slow, ominous tread of men laden with a burden; bearing with infinite care that which was well beyond hurting . . . ." It is painfully evident that Miss Ferber is frantically signaling her audience from out front. If she can only communicate to them beforehand what is coming, perhaps she can get the audience to create the scene for themselves. In order to cover her tracks and make the audience believe that she has given them a deep insight into human nature, Miss Ferber says, dipping into the handbook of popular psychology: "Selina had never heard that sound before, and yet, hearing it, she recognized it by one of those pangs, centuries old, called woman's instinct." Now Miss Ferber calls for her sound effects: "Thud—shuffle—thud—shuffle— up the narrow stairway along the passage." This is Selina's cue; Miss Ferber can put her heroine through all the attitudes of stage horror and no one will notice that this experience has no visible effect upon Selina's emotions.

> Selina stood up, the needle poised in her hand. The hat fell to the floor. Her eyes were wide, fixed. Her lips slightly parted. The listening look. She knew . . . . Selina's suspended breath came back. She was panting now. She had flung open the door. A flat still burden covered with an overcoat carelessly flung over the face. The feet, in their squaretoed boots, wobbled listlessly. Selina noticed how shiny the boots were. He was always very finicking about such things.[11]

With Simeon Peake disposed of, Miss Ferber can summarize the action while Selina slips behind the scene and

[11] *So Big,* 14-15.

changes clothes for the next act. During this brief intermission the author steps forward and announces that "Simeon Peake had been shot in Jeff Hankins' place at five in the afternoon. The irony of it was that the bullet had not been intended for him at all." The real irony here is, of course, that contrary to the author's intentions, Selina has no reaction to her father's death. Selina merely notices with camera-like objectivity "how shiny his boots were." Then Miss Ferber gives us a wry little notice about that accidental bullet, so that Simeon Peake is forgotten and Selina marches on through life as though her father had never existed. Selina's incapacity for feeling is further revealed when her husband dies. Selina, being a practical business woman, refuses to mourn for her husband because she cannot afford the luxury of grief. Miss Ferber evidently believes that grief is an emotion that can be turned off at will.

But Selina's lack of feeling is, paradoxically, the only true note struck in this novel, though Miss Ferber doesn't notice it. If she had developed her heroine's story through scenes rather than through easy assertions, Selina Peake De-Jong might have developed into a convincing example of the successful business woman. As it is, however, Selina amounts to little more than a sentimental humbug.

So Big still appears on reading lists for high school students, although it has evidently lost its standing among academic critics. At least, one no longer finds it on lists of great American novels. In another fifty or seventy-five years, perhaps, historians of American literature will be able to invoke the title of Miss Ferber's novel as they now do Sara Payson Willis' *Fern Leaves From Fanny's Port-Folio*, that sentimental best seller of Hawthorne's day, because *So Big* will have come to signify the low level to which even educated American taste was capable of sinking in the 1920's.

In 1921, Sinclair Lewis would have accepted the Pulitzer prize for *Main Street* even after he had tried and failed to get it for *Free Air* in 1920, but after they "robbed" him of it in 1921 and again in 1923, he was determined to refuse it if it were offered him.[12] If that happened, he wrote his publisher, he planned to turn it down "with a polite but firm letter which I shall let the press have, and which ought to make it impossible for anyone ever to accept the novel prize (not the play or history prize) thereafter without acknowledging themselves as willing to sell out."[13] For six years, on and off, Lewis brooded over the wrong that had been done him, and planned the letter he would write if the Pulitzer authorities ever tried to give him their prize.

Almost a month before the 1926 prizes were to be announced, Lewis heard from his publisher, Harcourt, Brace and Company, that there was a good chance that *Arrowsmith* might take the Pulitzer prize, and Lewis wrote back asking for copies of a letter Robert Morss Lovett had written in 1921 "denouncing [the Pulitzer authorities]—giving away their turning down the 'committee of experts' on the matter of *Main Street.*"[14] He wanted to have his materials ready in case. A few days later, he heard again from another source that *Arrowsmith* would probably be the jury's choice, and he wrote Harcourt that he was "waiting the more eagerly for the dope which I asked you to send me."[15] On April 26, Lewis wrote again to say that he had been notified confidentially that *Arrowsmith* would be awarded the prize on May 3. He enclosed a draft of the letter of refusal which he proposed to

---

[12] *From Main Street to Stockholm; Letters of Sinclair Lewis, 1919–1930*, edited and with an introduction by Harrison Smith (New York, 1952), 203.

[13] *Ibid.*

[14] *Ibid.*, 203–204.

[15] *Ibid.*, 206.

send, and asked the Harcourt staff to go over it carefully.[16] Lewis rewrote the letter ("toned it down and cleaned it up") and on May 2 the new version was in his publisher's hands ready for release to the Associated Press, to *Publisher's Weekly*, and to "the weeklies and monthlies, our list of booksellers and clerks, and . . . a careful list of about a hundred authors, such as Dreiser, Sandburg, Anderson, Cather, Mencken, etc."[17]

On May 3, the event Lewis had dreamed about and brooded over during the past six years came to pass: Columbia University announced that the Pulitzer prize had been given him for his novel *Arrowsmith*. On May 5, the news of Lewis' refusal was on the front page of newspapers across the country. In his public letter addressed to the Pulitzer authorities, Lewis gave as his main reason for refusing the prize the temptation generated by such awards—they seduced a writer into forsaking the quest of literary excellence, and into catering to the whims of a "haphazard committee" whose standards were "whatever code of good form may chance to be popular at the moment." In time, he also added, such a body could become so powerful that for a writer to challenge it would be to "commit blasphemy."[18]

Lewis' reasons for turning down the Pulitzer prize were not taken very seriously, even by those who thought he had acted out of sincere conviction rather than, as some charged, from a desire to exploit himself.[19] No one, it was argued, would consciously set out to write a book in order to win a

[16] *Ibid.*, 10–11.
[17] *Ibid.*, 214.
[18] The full text of Lewis' letter of refusal was published in the *New York Times*, May 6, 1926, p. 1.
[19] Ralph Pulitzer, son of the founder and a member of the Advisory Board, was quoted as saying, "Mr. Lewis has the right to refuse any prize awards offered to him, whether he does so from principle or from self-exploitation" (*Ibid.*, 17).

literary prize.[20] Much of what Lewis said in his letter was merely rationalization for the hurt he felt at having been turned down for *Main Street*, of course, but it is also possible that, speaking for himself, he had not exaggerated the lure of literary prizes. The fact that he had brooded for so long about the *Main Street* injustice, planning the "polite but firm" letter he would write, shows how seriously he regarded it. And once the award had been tendered and his letter of refusal drafted, he felt the awful seriousness of what he was doing: ". . . my God, you can't refuse a thing like this without giving reasons and without having in that refusal a document which stands on its own feet, completely self-explanatory. . . . An asinine, fantastic, useless, expensive gesture, refusing this prize." Wouldn't the other prize winners be "sore"—especially Tarkington? Would his publisher think him insane? Well, his answer would be Luther's justification: "I can do no other."[21]

Even though Lewis rejected the prize and returned the $1,000 check, the Pulitzer officials refused to alter their decision. They had designated *Arrowsmith* as the prize novel of the year, and that was the way the record would stand.

One of the men responsible for giving *Arrowsmith* the prize in 1926 was Robert Morss Lovett, who had served on the 1921 jury when *Main Street* was rejected, and who had argued that Lewis' satire was implicitly idealistic.[22] It is not known whether any of the "conservative" jurors who disliked Lewis' earlier work were on the fiction jury in 1926, but if any had been, even they would have had difficulty in making a case against *Arrowsmith*. For, despite some occasional

20 *New York Times*, May 7, 1926, p. 19, and May 12, 1926, p. 27; "Literary Main Street," *Nation*, Vol. CXXII (May 19, 1926), 546; and "Sinclair Lewis' Gesture," *New Republic*, Vol. XLVI (May 19, 1926), 397.
21 *Main Street to Stockholm*, 209.
22 "Pulitzer Prize," *New Republic*, Vol. XXVII (June 22, 1921), 114.

satiric scenes, *Arrowsmith* is in large part explicitly idealistic. In science, and in the selfless devotion of the dedicated man of science, Lewis had at last found a hero and a point of view that he could hold up for sustained admiration.

The main plot of *Arrowsmith* deals with the lifelong struggle of Martin Arrowsmith to escape from the conventional and "practical" world into a realm where "pure" scientific research could be pursued. Lewis shows Martin Arrowsmith in medical school, in general practice in a small middle western town, as an assistant, and then as chief health commissioner in Nautilus, a larger middle western city. Everywhere Arrowsmith goes, the same thing happens. Because he tries to conform to the accepted pattern of behaviour, he always ends by compromising his scientific ideals. Eventually he leaves the Middle West and goes to New York to the great temple of science, McGurk Institute. There, he approaches the possibility of the perfect life: plugging along every day on his individualistic, impractical research on the "X-principle of the phage." But even at McGurk, there are pressures exerted by the "men of measured merriment" who are always willing to compromise the far-off, distant "Truth" for position, fame, and humanitarianism. Because of this pressure, Arrowsmith is at first distracted from his laboratory, but then, quite unexpectedly, he is given the opportunity of a lifetime. A plague has broken out in the West Indies and he is sent there to conduct a controlled experiment, giving inoculations to part of the population and withholding it from the rest. Suddenly, however, a personal tragedy overtakes him. His beloved wife, Leora, dies of the plague. Out of grief at her death and because of the suffering of the natives, Arrowsmith gives way to the arguments of humanitarianism; he relinquishes his "controls," and allows the phage to be given indiscriminately to one and all. Consequently, he receives

61

much favorable publicity, a new and rich wife, social position, and increased stature at McGurk. These material rewards, of course, conspire to corrupt Arrowsmith's truth-seeking. His new wife and her society friends find him fascinating and clutter up his laboratory. His superiors at McGurk try to force him to precipitate conclusions and easy glory. At the end of the novel, however, Arrowsmith revolts against the "men of measured merriment," and against the claims of his wife and infant son, and heads off to a laboratory in the Vermont woods, where he and a colleague are to work on a new quinine project. "I feel as if I were really beginning to work now," says Martin. "This new quinine stuff may prove pretty good. We'll plug along on it for two or three years, and maybe we'll get something permanent—and probably we'll fail!"[23]

Loosely fitted alongside the Martin Arrowsmith story is some more typical Lewis material, satiric passages in the old *Main Street-Babbitt* manner, which ridicule the follies, vanities, and stupidities of the society in which Arrowsmith tries to live and work and which conspire to defeat him. The principal object of Lewis' satire is Dr. Almus Pickerbaugh, health commissioner of Nautilus, a "booster" for health, and a writer of bad verse. He is the scientist turned clown, charlatan, and politician. His opposite is Dr. Max Gottlieb, who starts Martin Arrowsmith on the path to truth and who is mainly responsible for his frequent returns and for his eventual triumph. It is Pickerbaugh, among others, who tries to corrupt Arrowsmith into compromising his professional standards. These two men provide the poles between which Lewis' thesis turns.

Arrowsmith differs from the typical Pulitzer prize novel

[23] Lewis, *Arrowsmith* (New York, Harcourt, Brace & Co., 1925), 448. (All quotations are from this edition.)

in several ways. Unlike *So Big,* for instance, it does not sentimentalize poverty while celebrating economic individualism, nor does it glorify pioneering for its own sake, nor suggest, in the tradition of the rags-to-riches romance, that the hand of the boss's daughter is the highest reward to which a young man can aspire. It does not imply either that all work, so long as it involves physical toil, casts a glow of saintliness over the brow of the toiler. Lewis' hero is also an "individualist," but his enemy is society, or more accurately, the purveyors of society's materialistic values. At the ethical center of *Arrowsmith* stands, not a successful old pirate of the economic world, but an impoverished, devoted scientist, whose example Martin Arrowsmith follows, rejecting both the rich girl and the money that fate has handed him—or so it would seem at the end of the novel.

And yet, despite these significant differences, *Arrowsmith* is still closely related to the fiction of Booth Tarkington and of Edna Ferber. Someone has said that a successful Broadway play can be made by inverting currently popular conventions. And, in a way, the strategy of *Arrowsmith* depends upon such inversions. Instead of striving for the usual goals—money, fame, the boss's daughter—Arrowsmith fights to get free of these, but he doesn't quite succeed. He does not want wealth, but gets it anyway. He does not, as he later discovers, want the rich girl either, but he marries her and begets a son. He does not want fame and public glory, though these are pleasant to have, even if they interfere with his work. Going off to the Vermont woods to work in his laboratory, which may look at first like a Jamesian renunciation, is only a George Babbitt-like retreat, for it is not really a rejection of fame, wealth, or rich girl, but only a protracted vacation from the duties of husband and parent.

But what puts *Arrowsmith* firmly in the Pulitzer tradi-

63

tion is the journalistic quality of its art. *Arrowsmith* is not so much fiction as it is a fictionalized defense of the scientific discipline and an attack upon the different varieties of soft-headedness which hamper it. Lewis does not explore and develop the complexities of his characters, but rather, he uses the characters to comment on the world outside the novel. As a consequence, his characters, like those of Poole, Tarkington, and Edna Ferber, are stereotypes drawn from popular mythology. Max Gottlieb, for instance, is hardly more complex than the advertising image of the white-coated scientist bending over his microscope and test tubes—"a maker of long rows of figures, always realizing the presence of uncontrollable variables." And Dr. Pickerbaugh is nothing more than a parody of Lewis' own parody of the small-town booster, sentimental poet, politician, soft-headed father, faddist, and boob. He is a rather elaborate and tiresome joke. Both Gottlieb and Pickerbaugh are, of course, merely foils to Arrowsmith, and it is not too disturbing to find them remaining one-dimensional characters throughout the novel. But even Lewis' major characters seem rather flat and wooden, mainly because they are puppets acting out and speaking Lewis' ideas.

Consider, for example, the following lines put into the mouth of Leora, Arrowsmith's first wife, when he is in danger of being taken in by Pickerbaugh's health-campaign boosting:

"Just the same, my lad, I'm not going to help you fool yourself. You're not a booster. You're a lie-hunter. Funny, you'd think to hear about these lie-hunters, like Professor Gottlieb and your old Voltaire, they couldn't be fooled. But maybe they were like you: always trying to get away from the tiresome truth, always hoping to settle down and be rich, always selling their souls to the devil and then going and doublecrossing the poor devil."[24]

64

Here is the essential Lewis, the fictionalizing polemicist, the American (and thus, more deadly serious and middle-class) Voltaire. That this truth did not go unrecognized, even by one of the jurors who voted to give *Arrowsmith* the prize, testifies once more to the nature of the Pulitzer authorities' journalistic, almost anti-artistic orientation. Robert Morss Lovett said that the chief value of *Arrowsmith* is its ability to "de-bamboozle the American public." If Lewis has "sacrificed the reality of fiction," Lovett said, "it is in the interest of the reality of a public cause."[25]

Today, almost forty years later, when America is becoming ever more responsive to the claims made for "pure" scientific research, *Arrowsmith* may be thought by some critics to be even more significant and "vital" than it appeared to Lovett in 1927. But however useful *Arrowsmith* may be in de-bamboozling the public, the grounds upon which Lewis defends "pure" science can hardly give comfort to any thoughtful person. In beating the drum for scientific research, Lewis seems to argue (despite Arrowsmith's humanitarian actions during the plague episode) that the scientist must ignore all human considerations, personal and social. Even Leora is valued by Arrowsmith mainly because she is useful. She relieves Martin of his loneliness and makes his life comfortable so that he can go to the laboratory to work on the X-principle of phage. Although Martin, we are

[24] Pages 218-19.
[25] *Book Review Digest* (1925), pp. 405-407. A criticism of Lewis by T. K. Whipple seems to apply especially to *Arrowsmith*: "Lewis seems to aim at much the same stage of mental development as the movies, which is said to be the average of fourteen. His manner is founded on the best uses of salesmanship, publicity, and advertising. It is heavily playful and vivacious, highly and crudely colored, brisk and snappy. He avails himself of all the stock tricks of a reporter to give a fillip to jaded attention." Quoted by Fred L. Pattee, *The New American Literature, 1890-1930* (New York, 1930), 345. Stuart Pratt Sherman and Joseph Wood Krutch, however, praised *Arrowsmith* for its literary qualities.

told, passionately loves Leora, he comes to look on her objectively: "He pondered on her as he pondered on the Phage; he weightily decided that he had neglected her, and weightily he started right in to be a good husband."[26] Leora, however, does not want to be anything more than a stepping stone to the altar of science:

> "You look here, Sandy Arrowsmith! Quit bullying me! You want the luxury of harrowing yourself by thinking what a poor, bawling, wretched, story-book wife I am. You're working up to becoming perfectly miserable, if you can't enjoy being miserable . . . . It would be terrible, when we got back to New York, if you did get on the job and devoted yourself to showing me a good time . . . . No, please! You're dear and good, but you're so bossy that I've always got to be whatever *you* want, even if it's lonely.[27]

But Leora enjoys her lonely life because she is cut out to illustrate Lewis' notion of the way women ought to be. He is so preoccupied with his thesis about science that he fails to note what a callow egoist he has made his hero.

It is in his portrait of Max Gottlieb, however, that Lewis' thesis becomes most explicit and most vulnerable. Lewis tells us that Dr. Gottlieb "casually, between two days . . . married (as he might have bought a coat or hired a housekeeper) the patient and wordless daughter of a Gentile merchant."[28] And, at the time Martin is about to embark on his trip to the West Indies to test his phage, Gottlieb is made to say, "You must not be just a good doctor at St. Hubert. You must pity, oh, so much the generation after generation yet to come that you can refuse to let yourself indulge in pity for the men you will see dying."[29] Martin is unable to insulate himself from

[26] Page 371.
[27] Pages 371–72.

[28] Page 126.
[29] Page 367.

66

pity after Leora's death, but Lewis clearly indicates that this is a regrettable and momentary defection. He means to show in the story of Martin Arrowsmith the final triumph of the pure, disinterested seeker-after-truth over the claims of humanitarians, medical quacks, religious hypocrites, demanding wives, sweethearts, and children. What *Arrowsmith* actually shows, unintentionally of course, is that a man cannot at the same time be a complete human being and an ideal seeker-after-truth who must dissociate himself from his own humanity. This is the same conclusion Robert Penn Warren was to come to in his Pulitzer prize novel, *All the King's Men*; but Warren's ironies were to be conscious.[30]

In giving the 1926 prize to Sinclair Lewis for *Arrowsmith*, the Pulitzer authorities passed over Theodore Dreiser's *An American Tragedy*, and F. Scott Fitzgerald's *The Great Gatsby*.

[30] See Chapter VI, p. 135 below.

CHAPTER FOUR

New Themes: Sex and Libertinism

THE AWARD TO *Arrowsmith* marked the beginning of a shift in Pulitzer taste. The authorities, of course, did not begin to favor works idealizing scientists and other disinterested seekers-after-truth, but beginning in 1926 they turned away, for a time at least, from their earlier preference for novels dealing with economic individualism. This theme would be popular again a few years later, but from 1927 through 1932, the Pulitzer prize most frequently went to novels that focused on the changing attitude of the younger generation toward love, marriage, and sexual freedom.[1] The post-World War I revolution in American manners and sexual mores, it seems, had reached the level at which Pulitzer prize decisions were made. This is indicated by the "realistic" manner with which passion could now be treated, even in books the authorities adjudged respectable. As early as 1924, Edna Ferber had described rather daringly the overwhelming passion of Selina Peake for Pervus DeJong, though Selina was, of course, terrified by her feelings and tried to suppress them. The dangers of sexual license, however, were not Edna Ferber's concern. In order for that

---

[1] The changes in American manners during this period are touched on by many historians and writers. The most thorough and vivid account appears to be Frederick Lewis Allen, *Only Yesterday* (New York, 1931), 88–122.

to become a fit subject for the Pulitzer canon, the social revolution had to proceed so far that respectable novelists could not only mention legitimate passion, but could treat in shuddery detail clandestine relationships.

By 1927 the revolution in manners had passed the stage where it could be ignored. At least, in 1927, the fiction jury selected as its prize novel a work that dealt at length with such matters as sexual repression, frigidity, and adultery— the latter of which was to be a major preoccupation of Pulitzer fictionalists for about the next five years, during which time the moral revolution would have rolled on so far that the prize novels could present, with considerable warmth and without condemnation, love affairs that lay outside the bounds of ordinary, conventionally respectable behavior.

The seriousness with which Pulitzer judges regarded these changes in manners and morals may perhaps be indicated by the entries Hamlin Garland reports as having made in his diary in 1920.

We are at a time when religion no longer guides and decency is in contempt. Family life is sacrificed to the cafe, the automobile, the theater, and the dance hall. We are taking on the worst phases of European life. The pursuit of pleasure, not happiness, leads to increasingly frequent divorce and "escapades" (as they are delicately called) fill the newspapers. It is the fashion for women to drink, smoke, and swear. Roadhouse manners are smart . . . . I am old-fashioned enough to be saddened and dismayed by this reversal to barnyard morality. It is a return to a lower level of social life.[2]

Like other writers and critics of his generation, Garland was also alarmed at the appearance of this "barnyard morality" in American literature. He deplored the preoccupation of certain young writers with the sexual side of life. "Love in

[2] *My Friendly Contemporaries* (New York, 1932), 366.

their books is raw animalism, instant in its demands," he said. "Their lack of restraint, their insistence on dissolute heroines, is not American but European." Garland despised what he thought were the motives behind this "literature of incest, adultery," which he found increasingly prevalent and he applauded the men and women who "took a whack at it" in literature.[3] It is not surprising, then, that given their particular moral sense and literary standards, in 1927 the Pulitzer jurors passed over Hemingway's *The Sun Also Rises* and Faulkner's *Soldiers' Pay*, although it is more difficult to understand why Elizabeth Madox Roberts' fine novel, *The Time of Man*, which could have given no such grounds for disapproval, was not chosen for the prize.

Hamlin Garland did not serve on the fiction jury in 1927, but he would doubtless have read with pleasure the book to which the Pulitzer prize was given that year, *Early Autumn: A Story of a Lady*, by Louis Bromfield.[4] For though *Early Autumn* does not "take a whack" at "literature of incest," it might have seemed an effective answer to writers on both sides of the Atlantic—James Joyce, D. H. Lawrence, Sherwood Anderson, and Ernest Hemingway—who clearly did not share Garland's concepts of decency, morality, and civilized restraint. In *Early Autumn*, Bromfield depicts the decline and fall of the Pentlands, an old New England family. The history of the Pentland dynasty in part parallels and is in part a defection from the gospel of rugged individualism, though the Pentland's fall is brought on mainly by the growth of sexual abnormalities. On one side are Mrs. John Pentland, who collapses on her wedding day and remains a helpless psychopath ever after, and her son, Anson,

---

[3] *Ibid.*, 177, 382.
[4] The novel jury in 1927: Richard Burton, chairman; Robert Morss Lovett, Jefferson B. Fletcher.

who is impotent, overly proud of his aristocratic lineage, and devoted to charities and scholarly research (he is writing a history of the Pentland Family, and the Massachusetts Bay Colony). On the other side is Sabine, a Puritan woman turned libertine. Bromfield shows that for all her emancipation, Sabine is a hard, bitter, unfeeling harridan. Between Anson and Sabine, at the moral center of the novel, is Bromfield's "lady," Olivia Pentland, wife of Anson. Because her husband is a Puritan, and because she is a woman of passionate, tender feelings, Olivia is naturally attracted to masculine companionship outside her home. Indeed, she falls in love with an Irish politician named O'Hara, who though somewhat "cheap," is on his way up in the world. The plot, as well as the moral drama of *Early Autumn*, turns about the question of Olivia's moral stamina. Will she succumb to the charms of O'Hara, or will she remain true to her marriage vows, and to the old conception of a "lady?"

After some protracted hesitations and soul-searchings, Olivia concludes that she cannot deny her marriage vows. Libertinism is not for her! Bromfield, however, provides vicarious consolation: Sybil, Olivia and Anson's daughter, is permitted to elope with the illegitimate son of a New England woman and a French aristocrat. This is an alliance connived at by Olivia to frustrate Anson's plan to marry Sybil to the son of another old and equally repressed New England family. The social message of *Early Autumn* is painfully clear: sexual repression is to be deplored, but frigidity in one's mate is no excuse for libertinism. Given time, the corrective force of history, and the old order will change for the better.

Early Autumn is another wooden imitation of the family, social-historical novels that were so popular around the turn of the century. Like Booth Tarkington and Edna

Ferber before him, Bromfield manipulates stereotypes as though he were writing a script for a Hollywood movie, calling for certain scenes and "shots" of his characters and their settings. Their houses ("Georgian . . . of solid brick"), their furniture (antiques, formerly owned by Lowell and Longfellow), their estates, their clothing, their conversation—all combine to produce something that reminds one of Galsworthy's social histories. Actually, all Bromfield manages is a patently bogus evocation of a region and a class about which he knows very little at firsthand. Further, like Booth Tarkington and Edna Ferber, Bromfield is at his best only when he is describing the outside of people and buildings as seen at a distance. When he is trying to deal with inner experience, his inability to go beyond exteriors betrays him. He remains, always, merely a reporter. Here, for instance, is a sample of his attempt to deal with Olivia's inner experiences:

> There were times when the memories of Olivia's youth seemed to sharpen suddenly and sweep in upon her, overwhelming all sense of the present, times when she wanted suddenly and fiercely to step back into that far off past which had seemed then an unhappy thing; and these were the times when she felt most lonely, the times when she knew how completely, with the passing of years, she had drawn into herself; it was a process of protection like a tortoise drawing in its head . . . . At the sight of him and the sound of his voice Olivia experienced a sudden blinding flash of intuition that illuminated the whole train of their conversation.[5]

To adapt a remark of Allen Tate's, it is always easy for a novelist to *say* that a character has a "sudden blinding flash of intuition"; it is quite another matter to dramatize that

[5] *Early Autumn; A Story of A Lady* (New York, Frederick A. Stokes Co., 1926), 33.

blinding insight and make it *act*.[6] Olivia Pentland's alleged insight remains little more than the kind of easy statement with which Pulitzer novels usually abound. For readers incapable of distinguishing between moral seriousness and pious moralizing, *Early Autumn* might have seemed an effective answer to the criticism of Freudians and Menckenites. It might have seemed to meet them on their own grounds, making the devastating concession, "Yes, there is Puritanism in American life which results in the inordinate repression of human passion," and then seemed to have turned the tables by showing how an adopted daughter of old New England (who was a Middle Westerner and also half-Irish) could experience passion and yet have the strength of character to resist such temptation because it was immoral.

In telling a morally anti-Puritan story for his middlebrow audience, Bromfield, of course, oversimplifies the issue of passion and repression and reduces it to a collection of clichés. His Puritans are rich, idle, snobbish, and psychopathic; his "good" characters are busy, kindly, somewhat lowly-born, and sexually adjusted. Much the same kind of simplification resorted to by—again—Tarkington and Ferber. The only significant difference between *Early Autumn* and its predecessors is that it deals explicitly with the problems of sex, whereas earlier Pulitzer novelists ignored the subject or skirted around it. In fact, Bromfield's preoccupation is such that one might suppose before reaching the end of the book that its author was siding with an adulteress and condemning Puritanism. But Bromfield is not seriously concerned with a drama of passion and repression. He is simply exploiting a subject that, having been taboo in polite fiction

[6] "The Hovering Fly," *On the Limits of Poetry, Selected Essays: 1928–1948* (New York, 1948), 157.

prior to 1920, had become fashionable literary fare for the newly "emancipated." With that talent often found in popular middle-brow writers, of being able to slide easily over moral ambiguities, Bromfield manages to join moralizing with a kind of veiled sexuality, leaving his admirers the agreeable impression that he is both up-to-date artistically and yet staunchly moral.[7]

With very few serious works of fiction to choose among in 1928, the Pulitzer authorities selected for their fiction award *The Bridge of San Luis Rey*, by Thornton Wilder, a book that must be ranked among the top half-dozen or so competent novels to which these prizes have been given. Wilder's book purports to deal with the secret lives of five travelers who were simultaneously killed when "the finest bridge in all Peru broke" on "Friday noon, July the twentieth, 1714." Information about the five travelers, according to Wilder's account, was first gathered by a Brother Juniper, who collected factual data in an attempt to answer the question: "Why did this happen to *those* five? If there were any plan in the universe at all, if there were any pattern in a human life, surely it could be discovered mysteriously latent in those lives so suddenly cut off. Either we live by accident and die by accident, or we live by plan and die by plan." Brother Juniper never learned of the central passion in the lives of these five people in whom the answer to his question was locked, but he left behind an enormous book which found its way to the library of San Marco where "it lies between two great wooden covers collecting dust in a cupboard. It deals with one after another of the victims of the accident,

---

[7] A remark by Edmund Wilson about a later Bromfield novel can also be applied to *Early Autumn*: ". . . not a single stroke of wit, not a scene of effective drama, not a phrase of clean-minted expression, and hardly a moment of credible human behavior." *Classics and Commercials* (New York, 1950), 159.

cataloguing thousands of little facts and anecdotes and testimonies, and concluding with a dignified passage describing why God had settled upon that person and upon that day for His demonstration of wisdom." Wilder's narrator undertakes to answer the question raised by Brother Juniper, to show that for each of the five people involved in the bridge accident, Friday noon, July twentieth, 1714, was the best of all possible times to die—because that was the day on which that person was destined to be happier than he would ever again become.

Like most of the prize novels, *The Bridge of San Luis Rey* was a popular success. It was lavishly praised by reviewers and later converted into a successful motion picture.[8] In this case, however, a good portion of the praise and success are deserved. *The Bridge of San Luis Rey* is artfully constructed; there are no loose ends, no blind alleys or false leads, no lapses into vulgarity, or no wildly improbable assertions about the intellectual or moral profundity of the characters. Neither are there any obvious appeals to popular prejudices or any sermonizings in which personal morality is equated with financial success. These merits have not gone completely unrecognized by reputable critics. Edmund Wilson, for example, particularly admires Wilder's "felicity of style" which he says, "has nothing of the pose of the self-conscious effort to 'write beautifully,' of the professional beautiful writer," but is "felt through the whole of his work and as much in the conception of the characters and the development of the situations as in the structure of the sentences themselves."[9]

Almost any passage in *San Luis Rey* will demonstrate

[8] *Book Review Digest* (1927), p. 808.
[9] *Shores of Light* (New York, 1952), 388–89. *The Bridge of San Luis Rey* was also highly praised by Joseph Warren Beach, *The Modern Novel* (New York, 1932), 478.

what Wilson has called the "consummate felicity" of Wilder's imagery, as well as his simple clarity and consistency of style. Consider, for example, this description of the Marquesa's pilgrimage to Cluxambuqua:

> . . . a tranquil town, slow-moving and slow-smiling; a city of crystal air, cold as the springs that fed its many fountains; a city of bells, soft and musical and tuned to carry on with one another the happiest quarrels. If anything turned out for disappointment in the town of Cluxambuqua the grief was somehow assimilated by the overwhelming immanence of the Andes and by the weather of quiet joy that flowed in and about the side-streets. No sooner did the Marquesa see from a distance the white walls of this town perched on the knees of the highest peaks than her fingers were turning the beads and the busy prayers of her fright were cut short on her lips.[10]

A comparison of this passage with any of those already cited from other Pulitzer novels will clearly testify to Wilder's superior talent. But Wilder has important limitations too, and these can be seen when one compares his novel to one like F. Scott Fitzgerald's *The Great Gatsby*. Whereas in reading *The Great Gatsby* one forgets that Fitzgerald is a fine stylist, and is caught up by the sense of human life that is so powerfully evoked, one is never able while reading *San Luis Rey* to forget that Wilder is a fine writer. There is always the sense of being enclosed in a kind of literary never-never land where real social, moral, political, and personal issues do not obtain. In Wilder's novel, too, one never *feels* that the characters are human or that their triumphs and sorrows really matter to the author except in so far as these represent brightly colored fragments to be arranged and fitted into a skillfully executed design, a design that strikes one as having been too deliberately arrived at. Each of the book's five parts

[10] Passage quoted by Edmund Wilson, *The Shores of Light*, 389.

deals with the life of a traveler who is killed when the bridge collapses, and each part ends at the moment the character steps on the bridge. One feels that Wilder does not really believe in the religious fatalism his book proclaims, but that he is merely using this concept to give his material an aesthetic structure.[11] Further, Wilder, like other novelists so far considered, often resorts to the reportorial rather than the dramatic technique. Instead of dramatizing, or utilizing his almost poetic skill with imagery to suggest the inner life of his characters, he simply states the facts. Wilder merely *tells* us, for example, of the passionate oneness of two brothers:

> . . . just as resignation was a word insufficient to describe the spiritual change that came over the Marquesa de Montemayor on that night in the inn at Cluxambuqua, so *love* is inadequate to describe the tacit almost ashamed oneness of these brothers . . . . There existed a need of one another so terrible that it produced miracles as naturally as the charged air of a sultry day produces lightning. The brothers were scarcely aware of it themselves, but telepathy was a common occurrence in their lives, and when one returned home the other was always aware of it when his brother was several streets away.[12]

Such glib generalizations about frequent miracles and mental telepathy are unconvincing and embarrassing evasions of the novelist's responsibility to make both character and narrative interpenetrating aspects of one organic drama. And so, although Wilder's settings are nicely described and his narrative skillfully structured, his characters are often flat.

At times, this discrepancy is so obvious that even Wilder's smooth and felicitous style troubles the mind's ear. One begins to feel that its ingratiating mellifluence is de-

---

[11] Edmund Wilson points this out, too.

[12] *The Bridge of San Luis Rey* (New York, A. and C. Boni, 1927), 95–96.

signed in part to conceal deep artistic flaws. Perhaps Wilder falls into this situation because his themes, characters, and philosophic and moral commitments come not from experience and direct observation but from his reading, particularly it would seem, from the poetry of Robert Browning.[13] All novelists, good and bad, are, of course, influenced by other writers and are indebted to them for techniques, insights, and even situations and characters, but writers of the front rank have something of their own to offer, some individual attitude or response to life, some philosophical concept that is so deeply felt that it becomes the window through which the writer looks out on the world of experience. Wilder's book seems to say, for instance, that love, supposedly felt by all of his major characters for one other individual, is the spring within the spring that controls and modifies human behavior. Yet this idea does not seem to be implicit in Wilder's way of looking at human experience, for it seems only calculatedly adopted for the occasion and imposed from above. As a consequence of Wilder's inability to believe in his story, and despite all the art lavished on it, *The Bridge of San Luis Rey* is, as Q. D. Leavis remarks, "faultlessly dead."[14]

An interesting side issue of the 1928 award to the *Bridge of San Luis Rey* was the judges' clear violation of the terms under which the fiction prize was to be given: the prize was to be awarded a novel which (1) presented the "highest standard" of manners and manhood, and (2) dealt with exclusively American life. The award to Wilder's book, at the least, violated the second of these requirements. In past years (or so it seems) these conditions had sometimes been

[13] Wilson found influences of Marcel Proust on Wilder, but *San Luis Rey* seems rather obviously indebted to Robert Browning—for theme to "Pippa Passes," and for structure to *The Ring and the Book.*
[14] *Fiction and the Reading Public* (London, 1932), 36.

78

ignored; the judges voted for the book that seemed to them to be the best that had been published the preceding year.[15] As it turned out, however, the judgments of the novel jurors and the conditions of the donor's will seemed so nearly to correspond, in the public's mind at least, that no one could have charged the Pulitzer officials with contradicting their official standards.

Off and on, there had been a good deal of grumbling about the Pulitzer standards themselves, not only from Sinclair Lewis who felt he had twice deserved the prize—for *Main Street* and *Babbitt*—but also from critics and literary commentators.[16] That there was widespread discontent among writers is indicated by the remarks made in 1928 by the president of the Author's League during a talk given before a group that included members of the Pulitzer juries. According to one juror, the president of the Author's League "recited the original terms" of the awards and "then gave the names of recent winners, to the confusion of the juries," and evidently to the embarrassment of the trustees of Columbia University and the Advisory Board members.[17] At any rate, the Pulitzer officials later that same year altered the terms of the literature awards, making them less restrictively "American" and moralistic. The men who served on the 1929 jury were informed that henceforth the novel prize would be given "For the American novel published during the year, preferably one which shall best present the whole atmosphere of American life."[18]

Had the Pulitzer prize machinery run with its usual smoothness in 1929, and had the jury's first choice been con-

[15] *Stuart P. Sherman*, II, 400.
[16] See Chap. X below.
[17] Robert Morss Lovett, "Pulitzer Prize," *New Republic*, Vol. LX (Sept. 11, 1929), 100–101.
[18] *Ibid.*

firmed by the Advisory Board, there would have been, as it turned out, no real need to drop the "manners and manhood" clause, at least for that year. *Victim and Victor*, by John Oliver, which received a majority vote from the jury, is a mildly shocking piece about a deposed Episcopalian priest who is brokenhearted by his exile from the Church.[19] If not vigorously idealistic, *Victim and Victor* at least suited the old terms better than either of the other two "nominees," *Scarlet Sister Mary*, by Julia Peterkin, and *Boston*, by Upton Sinclair. But a month before the names of the prize winners were to be released, the chairman of the novel jury, Richard Burton, told an audience in Minneapolis that *Victim and Victor* was "a book not just for a year but for many years." *Publisher's Weekly*, taking Burton's remark as a hint that Oliver's novel would be the 1929 prize winner, published that hint as a certainty. Columbia University officials publicly denied that any final decision had been made or would be made "until the prize committee began its deliberation"; privately, they wrote Burton for the names of other titles which the jury had considered. Burton assured the Columbia authorities that *Scarlet Sister Mary* was "practically" the jury's second choice. Then the board members read Mrs. Peterkin's novel (so the *Times* reported), and voted to give the prize to it instead of to *Victim and Victor*.

At the time of its publication, *Scarlet Sister Mary* enjoyed a mild *succès de scandale* because the main character, a Negro woman, had seven illegitimate children. To say that the book is about a "scarlet" woman, however, is to put false emphasis upon its intention.[20] Mrs. Peterkin touches very lightly on the "affairs" of Mary and deals with the difficulties of her position—the loss of her husband to another woman,

[19] *New York Times*, April 17, 1929, p. 55, and May 17, 1929, p. 12.
[20] *Book Review Digest* (1928), pp. 612–13.

the subsequent grief from which she almost dies, the gradual development of a liaison with her husband's brother, and then the difficulties encountered in rearing her children. Toward the end of the novel, Mary experiences a religious conversion, repents of her past conduct, and is welcomed back to the band of "saints" at the Heaven's Gate Church.

Scarlet Sister Mary belongs definitely to the second phase of the Pulitzer novel history: "libertinism" is, in the proper way, admitted as a subject; it is clearly condemned by the author and is used in order to help define the "good." In this instance, sexual immorality (as many reviewers assured their readers) is excused because it is "typical" of the Negro race; and, in the kind of contradiction often found in these novels, because Mary repents and reforms in compliance to conventional white American middle-class morality. Despite its defects, however, Scarlet Sister Mary is more convincing than many of the prize novels. While it is not as sophisticated as Mrs. Wharton's The Age of Innocence nor as smoothly written or as well constructed as The Bridge of San Luis Rey, it seems to be derived, in part at least, from firsthand observation rather than mere daydreams.

Sometime after the award to Scarlet Sister Mary, the Pulitzer officials evidently concluded that the phrase "preferably . . . dealing with the whole of American life" was not sufficiently clear, and so "simply as a matter of clarity" decided to change the terms again. The new conditions provided that the 1930 award would be made: "For the best American novel published during the year, preferably one which shall best present the wholesome atmosphere of American life."[21] Though these new terms partially restored the moralism that had been swept out the previous year, they

[21] New York Times, Nov. 18, 1931, p. 25, and May 13, 1930, p. 1. See also footnote 16, Chapter I above.

at least gave the jurors official sanction for applying largely literary standards in selecting the next prize-winning book—had they wished to use them. This new liberty, however, had no perceptible effect on the next year's prize decision. Literary excellence remained, in the minds of the judges, inextricably linked with standards of conventional morality. The new terms merely resolved the old problem of whether morality was to be advanced only by presenting pictures of wholesome behavior, or whether it could also be advanced by the inclusions of some immoralities "morally" treated.

The 1930 Pulitzer judges, whoever they were, must have known that Hemingway's *A Farewell to Arms* was available for the prize. Even if they did not consider it suitably moral, they must have been aware that Hemingway's novel had called forth many favorable, even enthusiastic reviews, including one by Henry Seidel Canby in the *Saturday Review of Literature*.[22] The only significant dissenting voice had been Robert Herrick's petulant diatribe in *Bookman* which, significantly, dwelt on Catherine and Frederick's love affair, which Herrick referred to as "garbage."[23]

Since Herrick objected to the manner in which Hemingway rendered the passions of his lovers, it could have made little difference to him in his judgment of this book whether the hero and heroine were legally married, but to the Pulitzer judges that technicality would have appeared extremely important. A novel that presented, for the reader's *approval*, a physical love affair outside of marriage—no matter how many justifications were offered—was not likely to win the favorable notice of men who gave prizes to novels that condemned such relationships. The Pulitzer judges wanted their prize books to paint sex as a corrupting influence, even if

22 Vol. VI (Oct. 12, 1929), 231–32.
23 "What Is Dirt?" *Bookman*, Vol. LXX (Nov., 1929), 259.

lurid details had to be brought rather vividly into the picture. In short, whether consciously or not, they preferred books that gave the lie to such works as A *Farewell to Arms*, which maintains the unorthodox and romantic position that a powerful love affair is more important than the preservation of established social and sexual taboos, and the rejection was implicit, whether the book had artistic merit or not. Such thinking, at least, would seem to be behind the award of the 1930 Pulitzer prize to Oliver La Farge's *Laughing Boy*

Laughing Boy, a handsome, carefree Indian lad, is seduced by Slim Girl, a Navaho woman corrupted by white men's values. Because he grew up in a pure, Navaho community, Laughing Boy falls easily under the evil spell of Slim Girl's charms and forsakes the clean ways of his people. Beguiled by whisky and sex, he takes up life on the edge of a white settlement where, unknown to her young spouse, Slim Girl plies her nefarious trade. In spite of his declaration (in a prefatory note) that *Laughing Boy* is without serious implications, La Farge makes it clear in the novel that Slim Girl's vices are the same ones that have seduced "the" Indian from his beautiful, wholesome way of life. Slim Girl, in fact, represents the Indian in his present corrupt state. Underneath a hard layer of sophistication, Slim Girl longs to return to the simple ways of her people and to regain her lost innocence. Her marriage to Laughing Boy is deliberately calculated by her to achieve that purpose.

But instead of returning with Laughing Boy to his people, Slim Girl, corrupted by the desire for money, insists on living near the white settlement where she can secretly visit a white lover. Only when they have enough silver and turquoise to travel in style, she tells Laughing Boy, will they return to their own people. But one day as Slim Girl lies in the arms of her white man, Laughing Boy happens by, peers in the window, recognizes his wife and, as she is trying to escape, shoots an arrow through her arm. Later, back home, he repents of his rashness, forgives her, and demands that she return to his people. Slim Girl, now reformed, gladly packs their belongings, mounts her pony and, with Laughing Boy, rides north to his people. On the journey, ironic fate appears in the guise of a jilted suitor who shoots Slim Girl dead and makes his getaway. Laughing Boy dismounts and, in great sadness, buries the body of his beloved Slim Girl, according to his simple Indian rites. Then, under the cold winter sky, he rides sadly off to join his people.

Although there were probably other reasons why *Laughing Boy* was given the Pulitzer prize—for one thing it is "social history," about an aspect of the American scene hitherto untreated by Pulitzer novelists—undoubtedly two of the main attractions were La Farge's moralistic and highly oversimplified treatment of Indian-white relations, and his implicit condemnation of libertinism. *Laughing Boy* and *A Farewell to Arms* were published too close together for *Laughing Boy* to have been intended as an "answer" to Hemingway's book, but there are some interesting contrasts between these two novels. Both focus on an "illicit" love affair. Both end with the death of the heroine and the lonely exit of the hero—except, of course, that the reader is meant to savor the poetic justice of Slim Girl's death and to rejoice at Laughing Boy's unencumbered return to his people. Instead of making the love of his hero and heroine an ennobling relationship (as Hemingway does), LaFarge clearly suggests that the physical aspect of Slim Girl and Laughing Boy's affair is corrupting; this is shown when Slim Girl instructs Laughing Boy in the white man's art of kissing:

Then she kissed him. He did not understand it; her face sud-

84

denly near his, against his, distorted so close to his eyes, her eyes run together. He was held tightly, and something wet, at once hot and cool was against his mouth, with a tiny, fierce imprint of teeth. Vaguely he remembered hearing that Americans did this. He did not understand it; he had a feeling of messiness and disgust. He tried to move away, but she held him; he was pressed against the wall and the sheepskins. She was fastened onto him; he could feel all her body, it was entering into him. There was something uncontrolled, indecent about this. Everything became confused. A little flame ran along his veins. The world melted away under him, his body became water floating in air, all his life was in his lips, mouth to mouth and breath against his face. He shut his eyes. His arms were around her. Now, almost unwittingly, he began to return her kisses.[24]

Passion overcomes Laughing Boy's proper disgust. He falls.

While *Laughing Boy* is not all this bad—there are some mildly interesting passages describing the customs of the Navahos—most of the book is amateurish, betraying the hand of the novice who has picked up his techniques and insights from the movies and from women's magazine romances, replete with the usual marriage-counsellor jargon, stock language, and psychological cant:

Any married couple, no matter how perfect the match, will undergo a critical period of strain, and these two were no exception. For all the dances, winter was a hemmed-in time; repetitious days indoors were a searching test of companionship . . . . They were attempting a difficult thing. They needed not only to see occasional outsiders when they were apart, new faces made attractive by the mere fact that they break the sameness, but also the presence of a third person when they were together, that their solitude might retain its value, and

[24] La Farge, *Laughing Boy* (New York, The Literary Guild of America, 1929), 92–93. (All quotations are from this edition.)

85

their unity refresh itself from the sense of the outsider's foreignness.[25]

In addition to A *Farewell to Arms*, there had been in 1930 one other excellent candidate for the prize, *The Sound and the Fury*, by William Faulkner. Considering the structural and stylistic difficulties of this novel and the general critical fog that enshrouded Faulkner during the 1930's, it is hardly likely, of course, that it received serious consideration. For to have bestowed even that much recognition on so complex and unpopular a work would have required a discrimination far beyond that usually manifested by Pulitzer decisions. What makes the authorities' neglect of *The Sound and the Fury* especially ironic is that although the atmosphere of the Compson world is anything but wholesome, Faulkner's concern here, as in most of his novels, is ultimately a moral one. Moreover, Dilsey, who is surely one of the most virtuous characters in contemporary fiction, is both more convincing and more significant than La Farge's sentimentalized Indian.

Faulkner was eligible again in 1931 with *As I Lay Dying*, a book not likely to please readers seeking illustrations of how upper middle-class people should conduct themselves in loveless marriages. A book more calculated to provide that kind of satisfaction was the 1931 prize winner—Margaret Ayer Barnes's *The Years of Grace*, another "social-history," dealing with several generations of Chicago "aristocrats."

By setting her novel against the changing manners and morals of the times, Mrs. Barnes contrasts the "fine old past," when children respected their parents' wishes and married for life, to the chaotic present, when libertinism is rampant and children change partners in marriage as their mothers

[25] *Laughing Boy*, 211.

changed hats. Instead of concluding her book as Miss Ferber concludes *So Big*, by showing the triumph of the older America and the transference of its values to the young, Mrs. Barnes clearly implies that those days are gone forever and that the younger generation is steeped in "modernity," which equals sexual promiscuity and bohemianism. Despite this final tone of pessimism, the author still manages to find a cheerful note on which to end her book. Because she is not one to stand against the irresistible forces of history, she has her heroine reconcile herself to the fact that the clock cannot be turned back and that if one's children are disappointing, one may look to one's grandchildren.

Though *Years of Grace* has economic implications, it rather neatly follows in the track of *Early Autumn*, *Scarlet Sister Mary*, and *Laughing Boy*, focusing mainly on problems of marital infidelity. The husband of Jane Ward Carver, the book's heroine, is a banker, and though that does not completely condemn him in his author's eyes (as it did Dirk DeJong in Edna Ferber's), it is evidence of his low potential ability to make his marriage a deeply romantic adventure. Mrs. Barnes's ideal in the first part of the book is an artistic young Frenchman who lives in Chicago and teaches Jane to love art (a reversal of the situation in *So Big*); but at the end of the book, when Mrs. Barnes wishes to reconcile Jane with her dull banker husband (even though she has spent much of the book detailing the failure of their marriage), she has Jane go to Paris and discover her old beau, André, now a middle-aged roué. The manifestations of Jane's moral indignation are interesting because they show the level of taste and intelligence to which this book appeals:

> "André," she said solemnly, "you ought to snap out of all of this. Leave Paris. You've still got twenty years ahead of you."

André was smiling at her amusedly, but Jane was not abashed. "You ought to come back to the corn belt, André. I know that seems ridiculous but it's true. Come back to the corn belt and do a bronze of Lincoln. Spend a winter in Springfield, Illinois, and get to know the rail-splitter. It would do you good."[26]

This passage is not, or rather, the author does not mean this passage to be satire or parody. Like Selina, of *So Big*, the heroine of *Years of Grace* is a plain woman, irresistible to artistic young men, who, as she grows older, becomes more beautiful. Like Olivia Pentland of *Early Autumn*, "Plain" Jane Ward Carver (as her author frequently calls her) toys with the idea of adultery, of throwing over her dull conventional life in Chicago and running off to the South Seas with a bohemian musician, but after the refreshment which vicarious dalliance provides, she turns the young man away, with her jaw firmly set and tears welling up in her eyes. Duty to a loveless marriage, to the past, and to the belief that one must sacrifice personal happiness to the conventional manners of the early 1900's is the lesson that *Years of Grace* has to teach. Libertinism, non-American nude art, classical music, bohemianism, art-for-art's sake, and passion are found to be villainous, and are either dismissed or condemned. Conformity—to the wishes of parents, to a wife or a husband one does not love, and to children who are capricious and selfish—is one's obligation.

Without meaning to do so, of course, Mrs. Barnes explodes her own argument. She clearly shows in the early part of her novel that the young French artist is much more attractive to her heroine than the dull protobanker whom Jane marries out of a sense of duty. Also, Jane's parents are shown to be self-centered and slavishly conventional; and after her

26 *Years of Grace* (Boston & New York, Houghton Mifflin Co., 1930), 574.

88

marriage, Jane's husband, more in love with his bank than with Jane, treats her with indifference. Only André, and later Jimmy Trent, the bohemian musician, have any affection for Jane. Thus, late in the novel, in order to make her moral unravel properly, Mrs. Barnes must arbitrarily blacken her unconventional characters. André suddenly becomes the "typical" French artist. And Jimmy Trent is sent off to Germany where he is made, in a drunken stupor, to enlist in the German army. He dies fighting on the wrong side.

But these unprepared-for tricks of character manipulation are only the author's small arms. Mrs. Barnes most powerful weapon in her defense of Jane's behavior is money: by staying with her husband, Jane has a fine house and all the money she needs. Had she married André, she would have been supplanted by one of the Venuses he takes every year as his model. Had she married Jimmy Trent, she might have ended her life as the mistress of a penniless traitor. Jane's good fortune is pointed up by the example of Mrs. Jimmy Trent who is lucky to have gotten rid of Jimmy. Mrs. Trent, a playwright, confides to Jane that she started out writing art-for-art's sake plays, but she is over and done with that now. She is banking forty or fifty thousand dollars a year and has abandoned her little bohemian flat for a fine old New York house. Thus *Years of Grace*, with all its moralizing, turns out to be another tract on practical economics. Instead of advocating "up and doing," however, it invites the reader to admire the cozy advantages of having led a dull, safe life and arriving at old age with a comfortably fat bank account and a well-furnished house.

On November 18, 1931, it was announced in the *New York Times* that the Pulitzer authorities had again altered the terms of the novel award. From henceforth, it was said, the Pulitzer prize would be given to "the best novel of the year by an American author."[27] Here at last was clear, unequivocal authority for the jurors to invoke only literary standards in the selection of the prize novel—or so it might seem. The real reason, however, for this liberalizing of the prize conditions in 1931 was simply that the officials wanted to give the next year's prize to a book that had nothing overtly to do with the "wholesome atmosphere of American life." The 1932 prize winner was *The Good Earth*, by Pearl S. Buck.

But if the book is not about America, it is "American" in the Pulitzer way. *The Good Earth* is the story of how Wang Lung rises from his lowly position as a poor farmer to lordship of a great house; how his rich sons are softened by the idleness to which they are bred; and how the house of Wang will sink back into the poverty from which it arose, now that the great principle of honest toil has been forsaken. Thus, despite its Chinese setting, *The Good Earth* is another ethical-moral American drama acted out against the relentless cycle of history which raises up one generation and causes the downfall of the next. Wang, despite his epicanthic eye folds, is a first cousin to Selina DeJong and Major Amberson; and Wang's sons, like the sons of these Caucasian cousins, suffer from that atrophy of initiative which, we are given to believe, accompanies inherited wealth. But one difference between *The Good Earth* and its predecessors is that Wang himself becomes corrupted by his wealth and develops a taste for exotic foods and soft, yielding concubines. Pearl Buck's Pulitzer genius enables her to combine both the theses of libertinism and individualism. Before Wang dies, of course, he reforms and leaves the magnificent palace in which his sons and their wives quarrel over his wealth and their proper

[27] Nov. 18, 1931, p. 25.

place within the family hierarchy, and he goes back to the little farm from which he came.

Instead of resting her case solely on the virtues of renunciation, Mrs. Buck, like Edna Ferber, employs the land as a symbol of goodness. When Wang renounces riotous living and goes back to the farm, he automatically becomes virtuous. Contrariwise, his sons, who secretly plot to sell the land, clearly symbolize evil.

One can see why *The Good Earth* might have appealed to the Pulitzer jurors as it did to many other American readers in the early 1930's—before the effects of the depression went very deep or very far.[28] There was, first of all, the escapism offered by the exotic setting of far-off China, the lavish descriptions of poverty and famine which doubtless made the hard times at home seem a minor, transitory affair. Moreover, those inclined to seek a moral for a troubled nation did not need to probe very far below the surface of Mrs. Buck's narrative. In the rise and fall of her Chinese dynasties, one could discern the recent pattern of events at home, and perhaps one could find a guide for the future. Weren't the poverty and suffering of the 1930's a result of the extravagance of the 1920's, when America had strayed from the rocky path along which Americans had traditionally traveled, abandoning the old virtues—thrift, hard work, sobriety? As the career of Wang shows, such conduct leads to softness and moral flabbiness, and then to poverty and to hunger. One need only renounce the easy life and the primrose path, take up the hoe and shovel, and moral strength would come again, and every man would be saved.[29]

[28] See Merle Curti, *The Growth of American Thought* (2nd ed., New York, 1951), 742–49.

[29] *Book Review Digest* (1931), pp. 143–44. Most reviewers thought Mrs. Buck had written an "intimate and accurate picture of Chinese life

Although Mrs. Buck does not suggest that her novel is a tract for the times, anyone seeking simple answers to the problems facing the country in 1931—the growing unemployment, the bank failures, hunger, and bread lines—might have found in *The Good Earth* a very satisfying prescription: Go back to the land.

It is another interesting reflection of the times that instead of proclaiming that individualism leads to great wealth —as both Tarkington and Edna Ferber had—Mrs. Buck says, rather, that it leads to security and safety, not only for oneself but also for one's descendants. In this we have a clear presentiment of the next thematic phase of the Pulitzer novel. Another significant and somewhat more subtle difference between this prize book and some of the earlier ones is that it does not attempt to reconcile money-making and morality. Mrs. Buck shows that when Wang gets more land and more money than he needs and begins working so that he can leave the land, then his corruption is assured. This is rather simpleminded, since it makes corruption depend upon the mere possession of wealth rather than upon character, but it is at least consistent with the moral vision of the rest of the novel. Mrs. Buck does not extol rugged individualism one moment and poverty the next, as do both Booth Tarkington and Edna Ferber. And though *The Good Earth* is sentimental and rather too patly idealistic, it manages to avoid the callowness of *Years of Grace*.

But in spite of its consistency and good intentions, *The Good Earth* is a childishly simple book in which good and evil are neatly labeled. Mrs. Buck always stays outside her

---

and customs." A Korean reviewer, Younghill Kang, writing in *New Republic*, Vol. LXVII (July 1, 1931), 185, said, in effect, that although Mrs. Buck had reproduced surface details of Chinese life, philosophically *The Good Earth* was truer of life in the West than of China.

characters, judging them sympathetically, but at the same time from a superior and somewhat patronizing altitude. The book's unity of tone is a mark of its superiority over the typical Pulitzer novel, but the pompous style by which that unity is achieved is another of the book's serious limitations. Whatever is gained in smoothness and uniformity is lost by the author's inability to make real, to dramatize thought and feeling. Its "folk poetic" or "Biblical" rhythms give the narrative a kind of factitious authority for allowing mere statement to screen psychological abysses which the author is unable to bridge. At a crucial point in the narrative, for example, when Wang is about to quit his good life as a farmer and become an idle rich man, Mrs. Buck simply says: "Then Wang Lung took it into his head to eat dainty foods . . . ."[30] Mrs. Buck tries to make a sentence do what a better novelist would need half a novel to accomplish.

[30] *The Good Earth* (New York, The John Day Co., 1931), 312.

CHAPTER FIVE

New Brands of Individualism

S EX WAS NOW A permanent
part of the Pulitzer world-view, but by 1933 the reign of
"libertinism defeated" as the dominant theme in Pulitzer
fiction was ended, and the old preference for individualism
(but now drastically modified) was reasserted. Perhaps like
Jane Ward Carver at the end of *Years of Grace*, the Pulitzer
judges simply concluded that the revolution in American
manners and morals was irreversible and that there was little
point in tilting against the relentless cycles of historical
change. Or perhaps, more likely the deepening economic
crisis of the 1930's had begun to overshadow problems of
divorce and infidelity, and the individual battle against
economic adversity once again seemed the most significant
problem of the times.

For by 1932 it was beginning to be obvious even to
many habitually optimistic Americans that the country was
facing more than a brief economic dip such as had occurred
after World War I, and that the traditional American faith
in the efficacy of self-help was being seriously challenged.
Many conservatives, of course, never faltered in their belief
that prosperity would be dragged up out of the mire of
poverty if men would only work hard and keep up their
spirits. But it was difficult for a great many Americans, in-

cluding a considerable number of conservatives, to feel quite so certain that individual initiative still retained its old magic.[1] Even the Pulitzer decisions, reflecting the more liberal fringes of conservative opinion, began to manifest a critical attitude toward the more rugged forms of economic individualism.

During the early and middle 1930's then, as the depression deepened and the effects spread to more and more of the population, the excesses of the idle rich came in for some criticism, and a preference for a more modest form of individualism was mirrored in a number of Pulitzer decisions. The traditional faith in the powers of individual effort held fast, but instead of insisting that individualism led to wealth and power, as had Tarkington in *The Magnificent Ambersons* and Edna Ferber in *So Big*, several Pulitzer novelists of the 1930's advanced the idea that the best of such efforts produce a modest living, and the worst create fortunes for the few while impoverishing the many. There were exceptions, of course. Margaret Mitchell's *Gone With the Wind* (1936) went even farther than *So Big* in celebrating the glories of rugged individualism, although Mrs. Mitchell's economic and political views were to be fairly well camouflaged by the trappings of historical romance.

This new attitude toward individualism begins really with the *Good Earth* decision, for Mrs. Buck invites the reader to admire Wang Lung, not primarily because he is diligent and shrewd enough to amass a fortune, but because he has the sense to give up his riches and resume the simple life of a farmer. Also, Mrs. Buck implicitly criticizes the idle rich by contrasting them to the famished hordes of homeless peasants. The first Pulitzer novel overtly to insist that a too

[1] Curti, *The Growth of American Thought*, 717–22.

rugged form of individualism harmed others, however, was the 1933 prize winner, *The Store*, by T. S. Stribling.

Except that it happens to be set in the South of the 1880's, *The Store* is in outline much like the other Pulitzer social-history novels: it begins with a poverty-stricken individual's envying the rich people above him, moves on to the downfall of the decadent rich, and then shows the rise of the new individualist to the heights of moneyed glory. Before the Civil War, Miltiades Vaiden, Stribling's hero, was a nobody, ambitious to possess (impossible as it seemed) a big house with white columns in front, and with a beautiful young belle in the parlor. The War gives Miltiades his chance. First, it makes him a colonel, an honor which, although he performs no deeds of valor, confers prestige and power on him after the war. Second, it helps pull down the old cotton-plantation aristocracy that had snubbed him before the war, and creates a situation in which a fortune can be built up by storekeeping. This, in turn, makes it possible for him to acquire, not a plantation, now, but a farm. Miltiades finally gets the house with the white columns and the beautiful belle, but he gets them through cheating and duplicity. Miltiades steals forty thousand dollars' worth of his employer's cotton, sells it, and uses the cash to buy a farm, to build his mansion, and to marry the daughter of the lady he aspired to marry before the war, but whom he had jilted in order to marry another woman whom he mistakenly thought to be rich.

However, Miltiades soon finds himself in financial difficulty. According to the economic law, decadent rich man down, rugged new individualist up, Miltiades should fall. But like the ante bellum cotton planters before him, Miltiades frustrates the deterministic gods that run Stribling's universe: Miltiades sacrifices a Negro to save himself. He takes back the supplies and equipment he had provided his Negro tenants, who are his former mistress and her son, Toussaint. Being a hard-working, ambitious young man, Toussaint sues Miltiades for breach of contract. In order to protect Toussaint from the townspeople, who are outraged at the presumption of a Negro's suing a white man, the authorities lodge Toussaint in the county jail where, ironically, he is discovered by a mob looking for two white thieves. Toussaint (the French meaning of his name, "all holy," is not meant to be overlooked) is dragged out and Christ-like is hanged between the thieves. Miltiades (and the reader) then discover that Toussaint is Miltiades' son; again we are not to miss the implication ("Father, why has thou forsaken me?"). But Stribling tells us that Miltiades the pagan "pushed aside the strange affliction of a white man who has hanged his Negro son."

This crucifixion of Toussaint at the end of *The Store* is totally unconvincing. It is merely a device for ending the novel, for eliciting gratuitous sympathy for Toussaint, and for making an unprepared-for allegorical comment on Miltiades and what Miltiades is supposed to represent. It is also unconvincing because Stribling's over-all point of view is neither Christian nor moral, and also because throughout the body of the novel, Stribling is wholly unconcerned with Toussaint as a human being. Toussaint is simply the old stereotype—the "good" (i.e., hard-working) man—who, in this instance, is cheated of his opportunity to work and to rise in the world. Toussaint is not even permitted the individuality of a black skin, nor any inclinations or interests not associated with the economic role he is made to play. Toussaint asks only to be allowed to till the soil, to buy fertilizer with his own money, to rise economically, to go North and pass for a white man. At the end of the novel, the reader is called upon to sympathize with this blank-faced abstraction and identify it with the crucified Christ, but only with Christ the victim, not Christ the redeemer.

Clearly, Stribling belongs to the school of "new" Southern thinking which views the history of the South exclusively in economic terms. Miltiades' Snopes-like actions are presented with bland objectivity.[2] Miltiades, it would seem, is not personally responsible for any of his actions (at least Stribling does not indicate any such responsibility until almost the last line of the novel). He is merely a cog in the Southern economic machine which breaks down through a regrettable human failing—prejudice against the Negro. If this could be removed, or so it is implied, the Southern economy would hum along like the rest of the nation's, and the economic status of individuals, black and white, would rise or fall according to the mechanistically appointed rhythms of history.

All in all, *The Store* is only a little more impressive than the prize-winning novels of Tarkington, Edna Ferber, or Pearl Buck. Stribling has managed to assemble a number of scenes and situations that are interesting in themselves, and to render convincingly some of his minor characters, particularly the poor white farmer, Cady. But the form of the novel is loose, episodic, and mechanical; the characters act in a moral and psychological void in order to illustrate the author's thesis. Further, Stribling's style is ponderous and heavy-handed. He is fond of Latinate or semi-learned expressions ("hobbledehoy" for boy, "transverse street" for cross street, etc.), and is addicted to the handbook principle of mechanical variation (Miltiades' first wife is referred to as "the heavy wife," then "the fat woman," then a "fat

2 Byrom Dickens, "T. S. Stribling and the South," *Sewanee Rev.*, Vol. XLII (July–Sept., 1934), 339–49, condemned Faulkner and praised Stribling

person").[3] Simple ideas are awkwardly expressed; characters are described, and their thoughts stated with little regard for the implications or connotations of language. Stribling's method is, in short, the method of the popular journalist with a message to impart along with a bit of amusement.

The official announcement of the 1933 prize winners included the statement that *The Store* had been chosen because it "sustained interest," and presented a "convincing and comprehensive picture of life in an inland Southern community during the middle eighties of the last century."[4] Although no such announcement was made in 1934, it seems likely that the 1934 prize winner, a first novel by an amateur writer, *Lamb in His Bosom* (*Miss Lonelyhearts*, by Nathanael West was also available in 1934) was selected for similar reasons. *Lamb in His Bosom* was perhaps not as comprehensive in its sweep, but it combined two almost-new ingredients that were to be much favored by the Pulitzer authorities: an exciting plot and orthodox accounts of female hardihood on the frontier.

Caroline Miller, author of *Lamb in His Bosom*, sets the scene for her novel on the Georgia frontier in the period just before and just after the Civil War. She focuses on the minutiae of pioneer life: the raising of houses, the planting, plowing, harvesting of crops, the slaughter of animals, the curing of meats, the encounters with snakes and wild animals, and the innumerable sicknesses, injuries, and inconveniences

because "His objectivity makes him one of the best of the Southern novelists . . . his is one of the sanest pictures of the South to be presented by a Southern novelist."

[3] Stribling, *The Store* (Garden City, N.Y., Doubleday, Doran & Co., 1933). (All quotations are from this edition.)

[4] "Pulitzer Awards Announced," *Publ. Wkly.*, Vol. CXXIII (May 6, 1933), 1,475.

of a life bravely endured without the assistance of medical science or other comforts of modern life. Mrs. Miller also includes a "romance"—the love affair of Lias, son of the God-fearing Carver clan and Margot, a "scarlet woman." After a somewhat lingering description of Margot's scarlet qualities, the author reverses Margot's character and shows that beneath the "heavy black goods" which cover her "shimmering limbs that gave off warmth like comforting white fire," there beats no kinder heart on the Georgia frontier—unless it is that of Margot's sister-in-law, Cean Carver Smith, a rural American version of patient Griselda. Cean marries young Lonzo Smith, leaves her "pa" and "ma," and goes off into the woods with her husband to set up their own house and raise a family. Cean works in the field like a beast. She "births" her children and then rises up immediately to carry on the household chores. Once, after birthing her only son, she single-handedly fights off a wildcat. At other times she helps Lonzo butcher the animals she loves, doctors her children when they are sick or hurt, tends Lonzo after he carelessly cuts his leg with an ax, and takes upon herself the burden of their farm and the rearing of their children when Lonzo dies.

Like her predecessor, Selina Peake DeJong, Cean Carver Smith thrives in widowhood and arrives at the threshold of old age as cheerful and buoyant as a young girl. As a reward for her patience and devotion to duty, she is given a new husband who comes closer to fulfilling her dreams than had lumbering, careless Lonzo Smith. Cean's new lover is Dermid O'Connor, a jolly, happy-go-lucky Irish preacher, who falls under the spell of Cean's charms and will, if necessary, even give up his religion in order to possess her.

Lamb in His Bosom hardly deserves to be called a novel. It is a grab bag of incidents, purple passages, pious sentimentalizations, and melodrama—all loosely tied together by a chronological thread having to do with the lives of the Smith-Carver clan. The book reflects a certain amount of familiarity with the details of rural life, but little understanding or feeling for the characters or the quality of life described. Indeed, like so many Pulitzer novels, the principal quality—and one suspects the main appeal of this book—is a kind of soap opera wish fulfillment:

> Cean laid her head upon his breast and did not note that the hair upon it was nearly white. Cean did not remember, either, under the drifting tide of blossoms and green leaves as she leaned against the clean trunk of her crepe myrtle tree with her head on the breast of the minister of God-almighty. The touch of his naked lips on her mouth was a sweeter, more comforting thing than any sermon he had ever preached. Here was a new sacrament—a new way of tasting bread and wine for the remission of pain and death.
>
> Then she turned her face fearfully up to Dermid O'Connor's. "Dermid O'Connor! Hit mought be a sin fer me to find such pleasure in your kissin' me! Hit mought be carnality, moughtn't hit?"
>
> He laughed, with his eyes shooting blue fire upon her . . . .[5]

Although Caroline Miller does not explicitly relate the perils of her pioneer world to the grim actualities of American life in the 1930's, anyone on the lookout for fictional homilies could have made the connection himself. *Lamb in His Bosom* would have reminded any reader brought up on copybook maxims, and still able to pay $2.50 for a novel in 1934, that where there is a will there is a way, and that you only get out of life what you put into it. For despite the growing unemployment and the deepening poverty of farmers and unskilled laborers, there were still a good many Ameri-

[5] Miller, *Lamb in His Bosom* (New York, Harper & Bros., 1933), 322–23.

cans whom the depression had not touched too severely and who continued to believe that there was always work for a man if he really wanted it, and that only the spineless propped themselves up with a WPA shovel.

While most of the major writers of this period were dealing with the struggles and sufferings of complex individuals in a complicated world, the Pulitzer novelists had gone either to a sentimentalized past or to far-off places where life was more orderly and where men, relieved by historical perspective of such encumbrances as fear, lust, remorse, grief, despair, and sorrow, could behave in a neatly illustrative fashion. In 1935, however, the Pulitzer authorities selected a prize novel that had as its subject, not the quaint hardships of life in China, or on the remote American frontier—but rather life on an American farm in the midst of the depression. The 1935 prize winner, like so many Pulitzer novels, was the first fictional work of a young woman, *Now in November*, by Josephine Johnson.

Now in November is told in the first person by a young woman whose father, ruined in the crash, returns with his family to the farm where he grew up. Instead of plenty and abundance springing up under his hand, the land becomes parched and dry, the house goes up in flames, the mother dies of severe burns, the eldest daughter becomes insane, the narrator's suitor deserts her, and the father at last succumbs to senility. In spite of all this, the narrator comes to the conclusion that even though "love and the old faith" are gone, there

> . . . is the need and the desire left, and out of these hills they may come again. I cannot believe this is the end. Nor can I believe that death is more than the blindness of those living. And if this is only the consolation of a heart in its necessity, or

that easy faith born of despair, it does not matter since it gives us courage somehow to face the mornings. Which is as much as the heart can ask at times.[6]

Now in November was greatly admired by some reviewers for its "beautiful poetic" style. When contrasted with the prose of many Pulitzer novels, Miss Johnson's style does indeed seem extraordinarily sensitive. At its best, it has the power to evoke a sense of experience genuinely felt rather than wishfully thought:

> These years marked by the dark torment of adolescence—that time when a fallen nail unlifted or a tuft of sheep's wool is torture at night with fear and accusation. When dreams are portent or promise, and there is meaning and symbol in the crossing of two branches of a shadow's length . . . .[7]

But Miss Johnson's poetic style, interesting and unusual though it is, is not really suited to the kind of story she is telling.[8] There is a running conflict between the brutal facts of her character's lives and the soft dreamy quality of her language. The effect is as though one were to write "beautifully" about the mass killings of modern war. But there is another problem with Miss Johnson's style, one that is less immediately noticeable, but which is ultimately more damning. As so often happens, when an amateur author tries to be poetic, Miss Johnson often writes rhythmical nonsense. Consider, for example, this description of a landscape:

> The elms were thick with buds and brown-webbed across the sky. It was beautiful and barren in the pastures, and the walnuts

[6] Johnson, *Now in November* (New York, Simon & Schuster, 1934), 231.

[7] *Ibid.*, 34.

[8] *Book Review Digest* (1934), pp. 491–92. Of the thirteen reviews noted, all but one were "raves," including the one by John Cheever in *New Republic*.

made a kind of lavender-colored shadow, very clear. Things were strange and unrelated and made no pattern that a person could trace easily.[9]

If this passage is read critically and if one attempts to focus on its meaning, it breaks down into a series of vague phrases which are, in addition to being trite, also confused. If the pastures are "barren" where then are the "walnuts" that "made a kind of lavender-colored shadow, very clear?" Usage of "colored" is redundant, and "very clear," which hardly fits "shadow," merely pads out the rhythm. The final sentence with its concluding homey phrase ("no pattern that a person could trace easily") seems like a plea not to expect any coherence from what the author has just described.

It could not have been Miss Johnson's ingratiating style alone that won the votes of the Pulitzer judges in 1935, of course. The main appeal of *Now in November* must have been that optimistic ending. One can well imagine that after so many extraordinary calamities had befallen the narrator and her family this concluding sanguinariness would strike some readers as an answer to the "nihilism" and despair of writers such as T. S. Eliot and the novelists often lumped with him as "the wasteland school." In 1935, F. Scott Fitzgerald's *Tender Is the Night* was also eligible for the Pulitzer novel prize.

Steinbeck's *Tortilla Flat*, Faulkner's *Pylon*, Wolfe's *Of Time and the River*, and Ellen Glasgow's *Vein of Iron* were all available in 1936 when the Pulitzer authorities selected as their prize-winning novel another social history about the American frontier: *Honey in the Horn*, by H. L. Davis. Sinclair Lewis, who served on the fiction jury that year, made the nonsensical comment that it was a novel which really

[9] *Now in November*, 4.

expressed "a land and an age, and by expressing them, really created them."[10] The land was the Oregon country, and the age was the years between 1906 and 1908.

The central character of *Honey in the Horn* is Clay Calvert, a young man who becomes a fugitive from respectable society because out of innocence and goodheartedness, he helps a suspected murderer escape from jail. Clay's adventures, as he wanders over the Oregon territory, provide the framework upon which Davis hangs anecdotes, tall tales, and expository or "philosophical" digressions. The basic situation seems to owe something to *Huckleberry Finn*. Everywhere Clay goes, he finds meanness, duplicity, and cruelty. Instead of a good-natured Negro slave, his companion is first a sullen, bad-natured Indian and, later, a beautiful young woman. And instead of "lighting out" from society at the end of the novel, Clay takes his place permanently at the side of a beautiful young woman in a wagon-train community which is migrating to another part of the territory, a sentimental and unprepared-for resolution in the Tarkington tradition.

Honey in the Horn is derived from the debunking tradition of Sinclair Lewis and H. L. Mencken.[11] It is self-consciously naughty and unconventional. Davis satirizes human inconsistency and pokes fun at popular "prejudices." His Indians are ill-tempered and quarrelsome; his sympathetic women are usually as strong as men and accept murder as a

[10] Lewis' senseless remark about *Honey in the Horn* (*New York Times*, May 5, 1936, p. 18) seems to be a garbled version of Wilson Follett's comment on *Main Street*, in *The Modern Novel* (rev. ed., New York, 1923), *xxiii*: "It created reality, and, creating reality, it had the force of the accomplished deed rather than of the written word."

[11] Mencken, it is interesting to note, said that *Honey in the Horn* contained a "great deal that was shrewd and pungent to say . . . [and that it was said] to vast effect and in language full of brilliant colors and lovely rhythms." *Book Review Digest* (1935), pp. 249–50.

matter of course. Scholars, religious piety, nature poetry, labor unions, capitalists—all are "debunked" in a style and manner reminiscent of Mencken and Lewis. Here are some samples:

It was somewhat the same feeling that one struck in school-reader poetry, in which grateful acknowledgments for the mild spell were paid to skylarks and thrushes and linnets and a lot of assorted poultry that actually had nothing to do with the climate except to exploit it . . . .

He was a nice-looking man, a widower of around forty, very well-meaning and polite with everybody, and without any bad habits except his unbreakable addiction to religious conventicles. He had tried to break himself of them several times, but never with any success. One hallelujah was enough to start him off on a regular round of them, following wherever they went and stopping wherever they stopped until his money ran out. It was only in his more despondent moments that he would admit that the habit had harmed him.[12]

All in all, *Honey in the Horn* is little more than an extended joke, a compendium of tall tales, outrageous comments in a huffing-puffing, chest-thumping style, the main point of which is mildly to shock and titillate the reader. Though some parts of the book are fairly well told, it is at last, as Mary McCarthy remarked, "a flat failure as a novel." And yet, *Honey in the Horn* seems somewhat out of place in the Pulitzer tradition. It is more amusing than Pulitzer novels usually are and it has no apparent moralistic purpose.

In 1937 the Pulitzer jury had available two very good novels from which to choose: Faulkner's *Absalom, Absalom!* and Dos Passos' *Big Money*. If these books were too difficult or experimental for the jurors' taste, there was also Santa-

12 Davis, *Honey in the Horn* (New York, Harper & Bros., 1935), 268.

yana's *The Last Puritan*, a good book that also had the virtue of being high on the best-seller list. But the Pulitzer jury had its sights fixed on the biggest of commercial big game: *Gone With the Wind*. It was the most discussed, the "largest," the most popular book of several decades, and these qualities doubtless weighed heavily in the jury's scales. And yet it would be a mistake to dismiss the award to *Gone With the Wind* as the apotheosis of the super-popular. The Pulitzer jurors doubtless thought they saw something important in Margaret Mitchell's historical romance—something that seemed to them wholesome, powerful, and fundamentally American. Edward Wagenknecht's comment on Scarlett O'Hara and the function of the historical novel in the 1930's may provide a possible clue as to what that something was:

> Many persons [in the 1930's] found themselves fighting as bitter a battle for survival as Scarlett O'Hara herself after the Civil War. It was exhilirating to watch Scarlett fight and win; even if she did not always employ the most genteel means, at least she did not lie down and die. Futilitarianism and deflating of values had been very smart during the 'twenties, when our economic future seemed secure, but they would not do now . . . . Americans more and more felt *the need of returning to the Rock Whence We were Hewn and of reexamining the basic postulates upon which American thinking and living had been based since the birth of the nation.* There were even times when the historical novel almost seemed to supply a "retreat" in the religious sense of the term, and when enlightenment, not swashbuckling, became the object of the quest.[13] [Italics mine]

What were those "basic postulates" re-examined in *Gone With the Wind?* Professor Wagenknecht does not say, but in explaining the psychological "need" which he believes *Gone With the Wind* supplied American audiences

---

[13] *Cavalcade of the American Novel* (New York, 1952), 425–26.

in the 1930's, he has put us on their track: "It was exhilarating to watch Scarlett fight and win: even if she did not always employ the most genteel means, at least she did not lie down and die." *Gone With the Wind,* in fact, is a story praising vicious individualism. The economic piracy sentimentalized and unconvincingly rebuked by Stribling in the 1934 prize winner is here romanticized and glamorized by Margaret Mitchell.

Unlike Miltiades Vaiden, who was a nobody before the Civil War, Scarlett is the daughter of a well-bred South Carolina mother and a rich self-made planter. The Civil War ruins the O'Haras and everyone but Scarlett is willing to slide into genteel poverty. Like Miltiades, Scarlett turns opportunist. She puts off the mask of the Southern aristocrat and takes to herself the role that had made her Irish immigrant father the success he had been before the war. But being a mere woman in a society that is bankrupt and still dominated by men who are either stupid or idealistic—and in any case ineffectual—Scarlett must use the only means available to her for saving the family plantation: sex. She will seduce her sister's fiance in order to get his money. To show that this decision is not an easy one for her heroine, Miss Mitchell has Scarlett fight a quick battle with the

> . . . three most binding ties of her soul—the memory of Ellen [her mother], the teachings of her religion and her love for Ashley. She knew that what she had in her mind must be hideous to her mother even in that warm faroff Heaven where she surely was. She knew that fornication was a mortal sin . . . . And she knew that loving Ashley as she did, her plan was doubly prostitution. But these things went down before the merciless coldness of her mind and the goad of desperation . . . . Religion forbade fornication on the pain of hell fire but if the

Church thought she was going to leave one stone unturned in saving Tara and saving her family from starving—well, let the Church bother about that. She wouldn't. At least, not now.[14]

Stribling, being a social historian, is unconcerned with such matters as sin and conscience. Miltiades' failings, he shows, are all economic ones. Miss Mitchell is a historian too, but she is writing for a more conventional audience and must answer or at least smooth away most of the potential objections her audience might make to Scarlett's unchristian behavior. Miss Mitchell's basic technique is visible in her creation of Scarlett O'Hara. Scarlett is presented as a strong-willed, overbearingly beautiful and passionate woman. Such a goddess clearly is a law unto herself. Readers who might themselves hesitate to indulge in such unchristian tactics as Scarlett employs, or thinks of employing, might nevertheless thrill at the sight of this beautiful, statuesque daughter of a Southern gentlewoman flinging aside the old inhibitions. And for more thoughtful readers who might find driving personal ambition insufficient basis for immoral action, Miss Mitchell provides an intellectual rationale: history. Scarlett, like other successful Pulitzer individualists before her, is, in part, a child of the times. She does what under the circumstances must be done if she is to succeed. Pioneer times have come to the South again and gentility will not do. Grandma Fontaine, who remembers the days prior to the war and before her family became aristocrats, gives Scarlett the formula for survival and supplies the rationale for Scarlett's tooth-and-fang code of morality:

We play along with lesser folks and we take what we can get from them. And when we're strong enough, we kick the necks

[14] Mitchell, *Gone With the Wind* (New York, Macmillan Co., 1936), 541–42. (All quotations are from this edition.)

of the folks whose necks we've climbed over. That, my child, is the secret of survival.[15]

Scarlett, too, refuses to be one of the lesser folks. She wants not only to survive, but to prevail and will use any means at hand to gain her ends—charm, sex, and, when she gets it, money. And Scarlett wins—wins the economic battle at least, though she loses the battle of the heart. Before the book is over and Rhett Butler walks out of her life, there are many stormy scenes in which Scarlett, rocked by tempestuous emotions, is pulled between her love for the weak, idealistic Ashley Wilkes (i.e., the old South) and self-seeking Rhett Butler, the war profiteer and adventurer (i.e., the new South). Scarlett realizes finally that it is not Ashley she loves but rather her counterpart—dynamic, opportunistic Rhett.

Before the final curtain comes down, however, Rhett Butler's character is given a thick coating of whitewash. He is endowed with a hitherto unsuspected tragic past, the useful foreknowledge that the South will lose the war (more historical justification!), and a deep, though hidden feeling of patriotism for his native region. When it becomes apparent to everyone else that the South is going to lose the war, then for some unexplained reason Rhett enlists in the Confederate Army. After the war, for equally unaccounted-for reasons, he generously donates some of his gold (made by war profiteering) in order to drive the carpetbaggers out of the South. Rhett also wins his way into the good graces of conventional Atlanta ladies (and no doubt conventional ladies everywhere) by becoming a model family man. In a way, he is, at the end of the book, the society-preserving "woman" of the novel, and Scarlett is the ruthless, go-getting "male." As Rhett Butler storms out of Scarlett's presence, Scarlett stands

[15] *Ibid.*, 716–17.

firm, though alone, determined to win back Rhett Butler's love and devotion.

It is an interesting coincidence that in *Absalom, Absalom!*, which appeared the same year as *Gone With the Wind*, Faulkner deals so differently with material that is similar to Margaret Mitchell's. Thomas Sutpen acquires a plantation, just as Scarlett O'Hara's father had. He too builds a house, buys slaves, and attempts to found a dynasty in the old Southern planter tradition. But Faulkner's "rugged individualist" fails in the execution of his grand design—not because of history—but because Sutpen's design, like Scarlett's, is based on injustice and brutality. Miss Mitchell goes to great lengths to justify Scarlett, but the justification is just a vast transparency of rationalization invented to excuse and glamorize piracy, coldly calculated self-interest, and violent disregard for basic human decency, all in the name of historical necessity and survival.

Some daily reviewers attempted to place *Gone With the Wind* in the "older" tradition of the English novel; but while one can hear distant echoes of Fielding, Thackeray (especially), and Emily Brontë in *Gone With the Wind*, Miss Mitchell's art most noisily proclaims its indebtedness to the literature of wish fulfillment—the bosomy and sub-pornographic historical romance, the sentimental novel, and the Hollywood extravaganza.[16] Scarlett O'Hara resembles *So Big*'s Selina DeJong more than she does *Vanity Fair*'s Becky Sharp. She is not a complex character, not even a type; she is a favorite inhabitant of the Pulitzer waxworks museum: the rugged individualist decked out in hoop skirt and organdy, and Hollywood make-up. Like Selina, Scarlett begins high on the economic ladder, falls through no fault of her own to the bottom rung, and from there begins the exhilarating toil

[16] *Book Review Digest* (1936), pp. 682–83.

111

that carries her once more to the top. Scarlett, of course, is not the sweet, folksy little lady that Selina was, but then public taste, dominated not by self-satisfaction now, but by anxiety, had changed considerably since 1925.

From 1938 to 1940, the pattern of Pulitzer decisions again altered somewhat. There continued to be a preference for best sellers and, to a lesser degree, for books which commented on the social scene, but the new prize winners were more smoothly written than many of their predecessors and they did not expound the gospel of hard work as the answer to personal and complex social problems. Whether the change came about because more sophisticated people were now serving on the juries, or because "serious" popular writers had learned more about the craft of fiction, is not clear. But that there was an improvement in taste during this brief period is reflected in the 1938 decision, when the authorities might have chosen Kenneth Roberts' best-selling historical romance, *Northwest Passage*, but selected instead a book with a more limited appeal, *The Late George Apley*, by John P. Marquand.

On the surface, Marquand's novel is the antithesis of Miss Mitchell's. Whereas her stock in trade is exciting adventure, Marquand deliberately dwells on the trivial details of lives measured out with coffee spoons. In *Gone With the Wind*, the bits of conservative philosophy and indirect comments on politics and economics only occasionally float to the surface from the deep deposits of unquestioned, violent assumptions upon which the romance is based. In *The Late George Apley*, the ideas are all on the surface. Indeed, one of the chief appeals of the book lies in the reader's ability to appreciate George Apley's political and social, literary and economic prejudices, most of which are conservative, genteel, and "aristocratic."

The main character of *Apley* is a thinly drawn composite of the "conservative mind" in reaction to the political and social events of the period between 1900 and 1933. The narrative device (the story is told ostensibly by an admirer of the hero) permits the reader to laugh at George Apley or sympathize with him, depending on the reader's own political beliefs and cultural background. George Apley, we are told, believes in individualism. Labor unions are bad because they are a violation of individual freedom. Prohibition is wrong for the same reason. Income taxes (on aristocratic wealth) and social security are "socialistic nonsense." The World War was a noble cause because it brought some life to old Boston and helped Britain ("our old home"), but the League of Nations is bad. The Sacco-Vanzetti decision is right. Alleviation of poverty and suffering are the duty of the upper classes, as are gifts to museums and genteel scholarship. Scott is a great writer. Sinclair Lewis is a "muckraker"; Hemingway is skillful, but a "trickster" and not a gentleman.

Although George Apley is a millionaire, he is not a believer in rugged individualism that leads to the acquisition of great wealth. He believes in the *status quo*. Great fortunes can be justified only if held in trust by the best families and used for the public good, and for the preservation and continuity of New England culture. The huge fortunes of the uneducated, vulgar, and newly rich should be taxed out of existence by the government. George Apley is also a firm believer in conservative manners and morals. He believes the older generation is superior to the younger. Like Hamlin Garland, he is shocked by the roadhouse manners of the young people and their casual attitude toward divorce and marriage. He deplores the falling away of the young men from the old Harvard traditions, delights in the English because they are "like us," and finds France the traditional source of vice and degeneracy where young men of Anglo-Saxon origins go to sow their wild oats.

Against the backdrop of history, Marquand's narrator sketches in the personal life of George Apley, who as a young man falls in love with a girl whose Irish origins are far beneath him socially. George gives up the girl in deference to his family's wishes. He is fond of the proper Bostonian girl he marries, though he has no deep feeling for her. Their marriage is dull, proper, and unsatisfying. For a time it appears that the novel is to be a serious criticism of the New England way, but toward the end of the book, Marquand shows that George Apley can do no other. The resolution of the marriage problem is, as in *Early Autumn*, to be historical: Apley's son is to break out of the mold, to marry the girl he loves, and to follow the profession of his choice even though it is alien to the Apley tradition.

Although *The Late George Apley* is sometimes read as a satiric portrait of a proper Bostonian—a reading encouraged by the use of a naïve and rather pedantic narrator—Marquand is not really critical of George Apley. Indeed, as Marquand himself remarks, *George Apley* is ultimately an apology for the New England way of life as represented by the Apley clan.[17] If George Apley is criticized, it is more for failing to live up to the achievement of his forebears than for being too conservative. This is to be seen in the contrast of Apley to his father and to his son. Marquand claims that except for the differences of manners, each New England generation is pretty much like the one before and the one

[17] "Introduction," *The Late George Apley: A Novel in Form of a Memoir.* (New York, Modern Library edition, 1940).

that comes after it. George's father was considered a rebel by his parents, just as George's son, John, is so considered by his. John's rebelliousness, of course, is not political; it is simply the traditional revolt of son against father. John enlists in the army as a private, refuses to join his father's clubs at Harvard, takes a job in New York in the advertising business, and marries a divorcee. George is shocked and hurt by his son's unorthodox behavior, but toward the end of his life he begins to see that underneath the different manners, the younger generation is not so different from the old. The chief difference is in the times. In support of George's conclusion, Marquand enlists the aid of the happy ending: John comes home from New York to take his place at the head of the Apley dynasty, and the divorcée turns out to be the daughter of an old and very proper Bostonian family.

While in many respects *The Late George Apley* might have been written to order for the Pulitzer prize, containing as it does so many of the favored ingredients, the book has one definitely anti-Pulitzer quality: it is genuinely snobbish and undemocratic. It defends conservative ideas along regional and class lines rather than along the lines of popular prejudices, although the mild satire, as well as the belated, democratic concessions of George Apley and the much greater changes in his son somewhat mitigate the snobbery. Further, *The Late George Apley* is not a sub-literary production concocted from Hollywood stereotypes. The style is literate and free of pretentious, journalistic clichés. The material is controlled and the story is not structured in terms of the black-and-white moralism usual in Pulitzer novels. Marquand's moderately commendable achievement is perhaps best summed up in Joseph Warren Beach's comments in *American Fiction, 1920–1940*. Professor Beach feels that Marquand has "a very respectable rank in American fiction" and that *Apley* is his most important novel; however, Marquand, Beach says,

> . . . is the one among all of these [important American] writers
> who might be felt to have picked his subjects not so much for
> their importance as for their smartness . . . . Marquand leaves
> us a trifle uncertain at how deep a level of his consciousness
> these subjects have taken root. This is not a question of intellectual so much as it is of emotional concern . . . one feels
> that . . . the author has said to himself not: Here is something
> I have got to get out of my system: but rather: Here is a damn
> good subject for comic treatment . . . .[18]

In 1939, the Pulitzer jury again by-passed the best serious fiction of the year (Faulkner's *The Unvanquished*, and Allen Tate's *The Fathers*) and selected the year's biggest best seller, Marjorie Kinnan Rawlings' *The Yearling*. The desire to get on the band wagon of a "big" winner was, again, not the only factor operating in this decision. *The Yearling* has many of the tested and true Pulitzer ingredients to recommend it. It is "local history" of pioneer life on the Florida frontier just after the Civil War, and like *The Able McLaughlins* and *Lamb in His Bosom*, it is packed with homely detail about the lives of the rude, backwoods people and their houses, husbandry, and speech. Interwoven with these picturesque details is the sentimental story of a boy named Jody who finds a new-born deer, domesticates it, dotes upon it, and finally allows his mother to destroy it for trampling down the family's crops. In a rather amateurish attempt to give her story implications larger than it can bear, Mrs. Rawlings, at the close of the book, tries to make the death of the yearling deer be symbolic of the end of Jody's boyhood: "Somewhere beyond the sink-hole, past the magnolia, under the live oaks,

[18] Pages 267–68, 270.

a boy and a yearling ran side by side and were gone forever." Although *The Yearling* does not drop to the level of such prize winners as *The Able McLaughlins* and *Lamb in His Bosom*, it is nevertheless too slight and sentimental to merit serious attention. Mrs. Rawlings' writing is generally amateurish. Her style owes much to Hemingway, but lacks Hemingway's precision and coherence of effect. Such artistic defects, of course, are not likely to bother the unsophisticated readers at whom the book seems, consciously or unconsciously, aimed. One can well imagine that, unlike many Pulitzer novels, *The Yearling* will over the years continue to attract young readers. As a review in *Time* magazine said, its permanent place will probably be in an "adolescent's library."[19]

During the early 1920's, when they were still relatively unknown to American audiences, the Pulitzer prizes were awarded in a somewhat inconspicuous manner. Checks and covering letters were mailed to the winning authors and brief announcements were given to the press. As the prizes became famous, however, the publicity became correspondingly elaborate. Beginning about 1927, the *New York Times* was regularly furnished with summaries of the prize works and with biographical sketches of the authors. Also, instead of mailing checks to the prize winners, the authorities summoned them to a formal dinner to which newspaper reporters and literary and academic celebrities were also invited. There, usually in a hotel dining room, amid the popping of flashbulbs, and sometimes before a radio microphone, Nicholas Murray Butler or some other Columbia University official would bestow the prizes.[20]

[19] Vol. XXXI (April 4, 1938), 69.
[20] *New York Times*, May 5, 1933, p. 13; May 4, 1937, p. 1; and May 24, 1939, p. 25.

In 1940, however, there was no public ceremony, no banquet, scarcely even an official announcement.[21] Shortly after the adjournment of the Advisory Board on May 7, a minor official of the university handed a paper to reporters which listed among the other prize winners the "distinguished" novel of 1940, John Steinbeck's *The Grapes of Wrath*. Although there may have been other causes for the lack of publicity in 1940, it is possible that the Columbia officials were embarrassed by the award to *The Grapes of Wrath*. As we know, President Butler was sensitive about public reaction to prize-winning books and if he felt that the jury had selected a work that would reflect unfavorably on the university, he was capable of having the decision overruled. The award to John Steinbeck for *Grapes of Wrath* was not overruled, but a statement that appeared in the *New York Times*, issued apparently by the university, suggests that President Butler was indeed unhappy with the award and apprehensive about public reaction. The *Times* account said that

. . . although the book was presumably judged solely on the basis of literary values, it was expected that because of the sociological and political significance it has attained since publication a year ago April 14, the selection would be attacked from some quarters as a tacit approval of the novel's disclosures by the advisory committee that recommended it and the trustees who approved the recommendation.[22]

This statement may have been the invention of a newspaper writer, but it sounds more like an official statement deliberately prepared in order to forestall criticism of the Advisory

21 *Ibid.*, May 7, 1940, p. 1. It was erroneously reported in the *New York Times* that no ceremonies had been held in 1939. But see *New York Times*, May 23, 1939, p. 25.
22 *Ibid.*

Board and Columbia University by making clear that approval was given only to the book's literary qualities and implying that the "sociological and political significance" had become attached to the book after it got out into the world.

But considering their anxiety in such matters, what would have attracted the Pulitzer people to Steinbeck's book in the first place? The answer is not far to seek. If one does ignore the book's political implications, any of the official reasons for giving an award to *The Good Earth, The Store,* or *The Yearling* as readily apply to *The Grapes of Wrath.* It might be said to have "epic sweep"; it is "social history"; it can be considered a "convincing and comprehensive picture of life" in Oklahoma and California during the great migrations of the 1930's. And despite what may have seemed to some readers to be an advocacy of government paternalism and labor unionism, Steinbeck's argument finally comes to rest upon a concept that is not foreign to the Pulitzer novel tradition. The Joads are not radicals spouting a revolutionary ideology; they are, as Clifton Fadiman assured the readers of the *New Yorker,* "a people of old American stock," deprived of their birth-right: "the privilege of working for a living."[23] Like Toussaint Vaiden in *The Store,* the Joads are dispossessed by social and political injustices. They are driven off their land in Oklahoma by the malefactors of great wealth and forced to seek their fortune among the migrant workers of California. There they are exploited by those who had arrived first and established laws to protect themselves. When the migrants attempt to organize in order to strike back at their oppressors, they are crucified (symbolized by the fate of Casy, the preacher), as was Stribling's Toussaint.

Thus, in *The Grapes of Wrath,* Steinbeck plays another

[23] Vol. XV (April 15, 1939), 81.

variation on an old Pulitzer theme: work is the solution to the ills at hand. In the 1920's, when times were good and jobs plentiful, Booth Tarkington and Edna Ferber showed that hard work brought happiness to the poor and discontented and riches to those with "get up and go." And in the early days of the depression, Pearl Buck and T. S. Stribling suggested that honest toil could bring security. Now, near the end of the depression, while agreeing with Buck and Stribling, Steinbeck makes the idea a tragic focus rather than an optimistic solution. That is, work would solve all woe, but work is unavailable.

The Grapes of Wrath was, of course, a better than average choice. The book does not attempt to mirror the only *true* American life nor does it retreat into historicism. Instead of offering a pat, moralistic solution to the protagonists' dilemma, the book simply presents the situation and, for the most part, permits the reader to draw his own conclusions. Altogether, except for the pretentious philosophizing in the expository interchapters, The Grapes of Wrath is fairly competent fiction. "Those sections . . . which remain free of large and false implications contain within themselves a remarkably well sustained narrative—held together by the simple but convincing structural device of U.S. Highway 66."[24] Nevertheless, the book has serious flaws. This is not the place for an extended criticism of so well-studied a novel as The Grapes of Wrath, but certain of the novel's defects, defects that are common in Pulitzer prize fiction, should be remarked on. For example, when Steinbeck tries to extend the implications of his theme through statement or symbol—as in the turtle incident, Casy's crucifixion, or Rose of Sharon's gesture at the novel's end—his narrative becomes forced and

[24] Frederick J. Hoffman, *The Modern Novel in America*, 1900–1950 (Chicago, 1951), 152.

stagey. And, "instead of emerging naturally and with due humility from the novel's material," the symbols are merely "added to it, or are singled out from it for special, self-conscious attention."[25] Steinbeck's characters sometimes seem contrived, too. They appear not to have seized upon their creator's imagination, but to have been deliberately constructed in order to illustrate the author's social theory. Also disturbing about *Grapes of Wrath* are the shifts of tone. When Steinbeck is dealing with the problem of injustice and oppression, his tone is outraged, but when he takes up the private lives of his characters, he becomes patronizing and sentimental. He exploits the Joads's idiosyncracies of speech and manner, their propensity for four-letter words and sex jokes, for purposes of ribald humor. While his humor keeps the social propaganda from becoming oppressive, Steinbeck's insensitivity to tone creates the impression that the "Okies" are merely useful support for the propaganda, or comic relief. One feels that Steinbeck is merely a detached observer looking down on his characters and their world. The humor, like that of Bret Harte (and of Steinbeck himself in *Tortilla Flat*) depends on the remote vantage point from which the characters are seen: it allows sympathy for their problems and laughter at their foibles, but by keeping them at a distance it prevents the author and the reader from taking them seriously as individual human beings.

Thus, although *The Grapes of Wrath* ranks high among the Pulitzer prize novels, perhaps it most belongs, as Malcolm Cowley has said, somewhere "very high in the category of great angry books like *Uncle Tom's Cabin* that have aroused a people to fight against intolerable wrongs."[26]

[25] *Ibid.*, 151.
[26] *New Republic*, Vol. XCVIII (May 3, 1939), 382–83.

CHAPTER SIX

The Fortunes of War

U NDER ITS TOP-HEAVY administrative superstructure, the Pulitzer prize machine teetered cautiously ahead, missing the best writers when they were doing their most significant work and catching up with them—occasionally if at all—when they were old, respectable, and, sometimes, dead. In 1941, the timorous course pursued by the Pulitzer authorities and the literary career of Ernest Hemingway, then in the first stages of decline, almost intersected: the Advisory Board, at the recommendation of its experts, voted to give the prize in fiction to Ernest Hemingway's *For Whom the Bell Tolls*. But Nicholas Murray Butler found the book offensive and forced the Board to change its vote. As a consequence of President Butler's interference, no fiction prize was given in 1941.[1]

An award to Ernest Hemingway in 1941 would not have been a very controversial decision. *For Whom the Bell Tolls* was not only a critical success, it was also a financial and a "moral" success as well.[2] While sales mounted (assisted by Book-of-the-Month subscriptions), reviewers and commentators hailed Hemingway's coming of age and welcomed him

[1] Krock, "In the Nation," *New York Times*, May 11, 1962, p. 30.
[2] See especially J. Donald Adams, "Speaking of Books," *New York Times*, Oct. 20, 1940, p. 1, and Clifton Fadiman, "Ernest Hemingway Crosses the Bridge," *New Yorker*, Vol. XVI (Oct. 26, 1940), 66–70.

back into the brotherhood of mankind. For Robert Jordan, unlike the proud individualists of earlier Hemingway books, had found a cause worthy of the last great sacrifice. Like Claude Wheeler in Willa Cather's *One of Ours* (a book Hemingway had panned in his earlier days), Jordan proudly faced the guns of the enemy.[3]

But in addition to all the current praise of Hemingway's literary achievement, there was also heard the usual gossip about Hemingway's latest sensational treatment of sex. It was this gossip, evidently, that came to the notice of Nicholas Murray Butler and determined him to keep *For Whom the Bell Tolls* from receiving a Pulitzer prize. When the Advisory Board, at its annual Friday meeting in May, voted on the prize winners, President Butler was unyielding in his opposition to *For Whom the Bell Tolls*. "None who were present at that board meeting," Arthur Krock wrote, twenty-one years later, "is likely to forget" Butler's "Olympian mien as he uttered the few words of adverse comment on this particular prize-recommendation: 'I hope you will reconsider before you ask the university to be associated with an award for a work of this nature.'" And since, as Krock remarked, Butler was honorary chairman of the Advisory Board and chairman in fact of the Columbia board of trustees, there was nothing for the Advisory Board to do but capitulate.[4]

The board members who had read the book found nothing offensive in it. They "had concluded," Krock said, "that the novel's literary quality and the power of the story it told overshadowed every other entry and met the purpose of a Pulitzer award for fiction written by an American and published in the year 1940."[5] Though not many reputable

[3] Chap. II above, and Edmund Wilson, "Emergence of Ernest Hemingway," in *The Shores of Light* (New York, 1952), 118.
[4] Krock, "In the Nation," *New York Times*, May 11, 1962, p. 30.
[5] *Ibid.*

critics today would agree that *For Whom the Bell Tolls* overshadows Faulkner's *The Hamlet,* which was also available in 1941, certainly it would have been one of the better choices in the forty-five year history of these prizes.

Another novelist whom the Pulitzer authorities had managed to ignore for many years was Ellen Glasgow, possibly because she was too genteel for the more "liberal" jurors, and too ironic for the conservative. By the time the Pulitzer authorities caught up with her, three years before her death, Ellen Glasgow had written a book that was somewhat more conventional than *Life and Gabriella,* which had been eligible for the first Pulitzer prize in 1917. It was this novel, finally, that got Miss Glasgow the Pulitzer prize: *In This Our Life.*

Ellen Glasgow is an important American novelist and deserved to win a Pulitzer prize. *In This Our Life,* however, is not a very good novel. It is the story of Asa Timberlake and his two grown daughters, Stanley and Roy, and their different ways of confronting life in a disordered, industrial society. Asa, the descendant of a once rich but now impoverished Southern family, works in a factory formerly owned by an ancestor. He is married to a woman he does not love, a bedridden hypochondriac who requires constant care, and from whom he longs to escape. Whenever it is possible, he spends the week end on a farm owned by the widow of an old friend. There are moments when he dreams of freedom, when he plans to leave his wife and become a farmhand. Asa's younger daughter, Stanley, is irresponsible and selfish, thinking only of her own sensual gratification. She is engaged to a young man named Craig, but she runs away with her sister's husband, a poor but promising doctor of medicine, and eventually drives him to suicide by her extravagance and selfishness.

Stanley then returns to the bosom of the family, where she is forgiven and taken in. An indulgent rich uncle buys her a car which she drives recklessly about town. One night she runs down a mother and child and drives away, letting suspicion fall on a young Negro, Parry, who sometimes drove her car to the garage. Everyone in the Timberlake family except Asa is willing to let the Negro boy go to jail rather than expose Stanley to the humiliation of a trial. After a struggle with his conscience, Asa notifies the authorities; Parry is released and Stanley is charged with the crime.

Through the older daughter, Roy, Miss Glasgow develops her theme about "our life." Like her father, Roy is clearly the victim of another's selfishness and self-indulgence. First she loses her husband to Stanley, and then she loses Craig, who had turned to Roy after Stanley jilted him. Upon hearing that Craig is still in love with her sister, Roy rushes out into the night and encounters a young Englishman on his way to enlist in the English army. They go to his borrowed apartment, but instead of turning "libertine," Roy merely talks with the young man and discovers that he "needed love more than she needed it, and was less likely to find it." This discovery "served as a flare of light in the dark of her own mind." On the dawn of the next day, Roy feels as "if she had overtaken time, and were walking into a new age and a new world." She returns home to pack her clothes, and in the kitchen she sees her father and cries out to him, "I want something to hold by! I want something good!" Her father answers, "You will find it, my child. You will find what you are looking for. It is there and you—not I—will find it." This conclusion is meant to put the final dramatic touch to Miss Glasgow's thesis: Roy represents the younger generation passionately in search of the "good," while Asa is the voice of the past, handing over to the present a hope for the unattainable in the future, which is, apparently, all that can sustain one in this life.

In This Our Life does possess fine qualities. Miss Glasgow's style, as one might expect, is smooth, highly literate, and carefully controlled. The characters have the virtue of consistency; what they say or do on one page fits into the total impression of their character as it finally emerges at the end of the book. Descriptions, scenes, and characters are functional, and whether or not one is convinced that the author has done justice to the complexities of life, she is not just exploiting a popular subject or following a fad. Virtue does not fall automatically onto the shoulders of her people because they wear a certain kind of clothing or because they are said to be happy on the land. She does not allow Roy Timberlake the dubious moral victory of toying with sensuality and then rejecting it through pride or fear of the consequences. Asa Timberlake's moral superiority consists in his refusal to put personal comfort and desire above what he considers to be the rights of others. He refrains from divorcing his wife as long as she needs him. He refuses to allow an innocent Negro boy to go to prison even though it may mean that his daughter will be imprisoned instead.

Nevertheless, like many of its Pulitzer predecessors, *In This Our Life* suffers from oversimplification. For one thing, it is an uninspired defense of the old-fashioned virtues of chastity, loyalty in marriage (regardless of what may come), honesty, sacrifice of personal desires, and selfless devotion to the welfare of others. While the defense of such things is certainly admissible in fiction, Miss Glasgow's method of defense is at last rickety and contrived. Further, though the characters are consistent and more subtly drawn than is usual in Pulitzer fiction, their actions do not develop them as much as they too simply illustrate and support the author's thesis. For example, Asa gives up his dream of retiring to the country, one feels, mainly because the author wishes him to illustrate the virtue of loyalty. Miss Glasgow's novel also suffers from the imperfect coincidence of her material and her theme. She intends the actions of Asa to sound the "stern accents of our unconquerable hope," but because she has shown how dull and thwarted are the lives of Asa and Roy, their gestures at the end of the novel are only weak and pathetic attempts to bolster themselves up with empty hopes. Thus, the major failing of *In This Our Life* is that Miss Glasgow leaves unexplored the ambiguous implications of Roy's and Asa's "victory in defeat," the sad ironies of their heroism. The author asks the reader to react optimistically without revealing what the grounds for optimism are. *In This Our Life* is a minor performance by an otherwise significant novelist.

The award to *In This Our Life* was made six months after the United States officially entered World War II. Miss Glasgow had touched on the war, but only incidentally, as a remote symbol of a disordered "world without moorings, and driven by unconscious fears toward the verge of catastrophe."[6] By May, 1943, when the next awards were given, the United States had been at war for almost a year and one-half, and public attitudes had changed from the prewar thankfulness that we were not involved in the fighting to a kind of outraged determination to beat the enemy, especially the "Japs" because of their sneak attack on Pearl Harbor. There was also abroad the less emotional attitude of wanting to get the job over, and the belief that every American, rich or poor, man

[6] Ellen Glasgow, *A Certain Measure* (New York, 1943), 256.

or woman, should do his part, if not in one of the services, then in the munitions factories, shipyards, USO, or the scrap drives.

Though wartime is traditionally uncongenial to the production of significant literature, during the period between 1942 and 1946 there was a fair abundance of quality fiction produced. In 1942, Faulkner's *Go Down, Moses* and James Gould Cozzens', *The Just and the Unjust* were published. In 1943, there was Robert Penn Warren's second novel, *At Heaven's Gate*; in 1944, Caroline Gordon's *The Women on the Porch*; and, in 1945, Glenway Wescott's *Apartment in Athens*. However, during these years, as might have been predicted, the Pulitzer authorities continued to avoid the best novels. In 1943 they by-passed *Go Down, Moses* which might have been disqualified as a collection of short fiction, but which could have been made to fit the conditions as readily as *The Bridge of San Luis Rey* had been, or as *Tales of the South Pacific* would be a few years later. The prize in 1943 was given to Upton Sinclair's melodrama about the Nazi rise to power, *Dragon's Teeth*.

Then, in 1944, the novel prize went to Martin Flavin's *Journey in the Dark*, a social history about a self-made multimillionaire who gives up his life of ease to work in a defense factory. In 1945 the prize was awarded to John Hersey's very popular best seller, *A Bell for Adano*, a sentimental tale of a kindly American major who procured a church bell for an occupied Italian town.[7] In 1946, when *Apartment in Athens* was available, the Pulitzer authorities voted to give no novel award.

Dragon's Teeth (1943), is a combination of wartime

---

[7] Malcolm Cowley wrote, "A candid report from behind the lines and an effective tract," and Diana Trilling said, "There is very little writing talent in *A Bell for Adano*." *Book Review Digest* (1944), pp. 344–45.

propaganda and Hollywood melodrama. Against the back-drop of Nazi politics in Germany, Sinclair tells the story of Lanny Budd, a well-meaning American who comes into conflict with members of the Nazi hierarchy by helping a Jewish friend escape from a concentration camp. This is all that can be said for the novel.

Journey in the Dark, the next award novel, is even worse. Flavin's book attempts, as one reviewer said, to "mirror a representative cross section of American life during the last sixty years."[8] But, like most Pulitzer social histories, *Journey in the Dark* turns out to be just another romance on the rags-to-riches theme. "Uncle" Sam Braden, as the author calls his hero, started out as a poor boy in Muscatine, Iowa. Fired by the ambition to be a millionaire, he fights his way to the top of the economic heap, makes five million dollars in a Chicago wallpaper business which he later buys (or practically steals) from the partner who had taken him into the business. Sam returns home to Iowa to woo Eileen, the town rich girl, whom he had worshipped from the other side of the tracks when he was a boy. Eileen is in love with a rich boy named Neill Wyatt, but marries Sam in order to spite Neill. Their marriage is cold and loveless. Then Eileen begins seeing Neill again, and when Sam discovers this, he divorces Eileen and, a little later, marries the daughter of a German couple he meets in Chicago. From their union comes a son, Hathaway, who grows up and becomes enamored of the half-Jewish daughter of Mitch, Sam's boyhood friend who had gone to Russia and temporarily fallen for the communist experiment. Sam opposes his son's involvement with Mitch's daughter (wrongly, Flavin implies, just as he had opposed the labor union in his wallpaper business years before), and he arranges to have Mitch deprived of his liberal newspaper,

[8] Clifton Fadiman, *New Yorker*, Vol. XIX (Oct. 23, 1943), 78.

which Sam had financed. Mitch is forced to leave town, but Hathaway marries Mitch's daughter anyway. Sam's wife becomes ill and dies. Meanwhile, World War II has broken out, and Hathaway enlists in the air force. Sam retires from his business and learns to use the lathe like a common workman. He makes a pair of steel dice for his son, with whom he has become reconciled. Before Hathaway goes overseas, Sam throws a seven and knows he will never see his son again. Later, Neill, son of Eileen and Neill Wyatt, who was in the same air crew as Hathaway, tells Sam what a hero his son had been and how much Hathaway had admired his father. Word comes to Sam that Eileen has returned to town, has given up her house to the USO and donated the iron fence (symbol of undemocratic class snobbery) to the scrap drive. The novel ends with Sam's going off to his lathe in the factory and being greeted by a fellow workman:

> "I missed you, Sam," he said. "You been sick or something?"
> "Yeh, sick—" He smiled. "I'm all right now."
> They walked along together.

In order to point up the meaning of his novel, Flavin has one of his characters tell Sam Braden:

> "You've done everything the copybooks advise, everything the kids are taught to think. You should be immortalized, for the story of your life is, in a way, the story of America—a statement of its *values.*—and now, from where you're sitting . . . a lonely man going no where, in the dark—"[9]

During almost all of his life, Sam follows the copybook maxims and makes his fortune, but he forgets the important American values of democratic "service" to others. The loss of his son apparently brings home to Sam the importance of

[9] Flavin, *Journey in the Dark* (New York, Harper & Bros., 1943), 376. (All quotations are from this edition.)

those values, for he gives up his luxurious way of life and takes up common toil for the good of all, without, of course, giving up his five million dollars.

Journey in the Dark gives rugged individualism an ineffectual little slap on the wrist; it is not a serious criticism of Sam's copybook success. It is a rather confused and incoherent apology couched in such vague abstractions that it is doubtful whether even the author knew exactly what he meant by Sam's story:

> He [Sam] did not mean, he said, to accuse himself uniquely, for it was his generation which must be indicted; he, himself, was no more than a reflection of the world in which he'd lived, not atypical at all. He could only be convicted of having realized the fruits which his fellowmen had coveted, of being a winner in a race in which, as it turned out, there were not any winners, since there were not any stakes—no *real* reward for winning; but only the winners had a chance to find that out. He would plead guilty to success—the very same pursuit in which most people lived and died, never knowing the stars at which they grasped were fireflies and marsh lights. And success had this advantage; once in your grasp you could examine it and appraise its actual value—a benefit denied to less successful men.[10]

The purpose of this passage appears to be the reconciliation of Sam's rugged individualism with his new dedication to service. By giving up his son, renouncing soft living, and rubbing shoulders with commoner men over a wartime lathe, Sam receives absolution for past omissions, just as his former wife is forgiven because she lends her house to the USO and contributes her iron fence to the scrap drive. The war sentiment in 1944 was the current solvent for irreconcilables, a new symbolism into which the most rugged form of individualism could be dipped for a coating of respectability.

[10] *Ibid.*, 420.

In quality, *Journey in the Dark* (which also won the Harper's novel prize) ranks somewhere near the bottom of the Pulitzer roster, perhaps below even *Laughing Boy*. It has nothing to recommend it. It is a series of badly written, disconnected incidents which the author attempts to force into significance. As a reviewer for the *New Republic* said, it is "smelling ripe for Hollywood . . . a popular novel in the very worst sense."[11]

After having awarded the prize to Hersey's super-sentimental short story, *A Bell for Adano* in 1945, and having given no prize in 1946, the Pulitzer authorities made, in 1947, what has since proved to be their best decision. They by-passed two big best sellers, *The Hucksters*, by Frederick Wakeman, and *B. F.'s Daughter*, by J. P. Marquand, to give the prize to Robert Penn Warren's *All the King's Men*, an unusually complex and only moderately popular novel. The main plot of Warren's novel deals with the rise of Willie Stark from a struggling country lawyer to governor of a Southern state, and of his fall from idealism to opportunism. *All the King's Men* is also the story of Jack Burden, Warren's narrator, for whom the struggle of Willie Stark and Adam Stanton is a projection of his own internal conflict and a symbolic enactment of a serious modern dilemma:

> As a student of history, Jack Burden could see that Adam Stanton, whom he came to call the man of idea, and Willie Stark, whom he came to call the man of fact, were doomed to destroy each other just as each was doomed to try to use the other and to yearn toward and try to become the other, because each was incomplete with the terrible division of their age.[12]

11 Vol. CIX (Nov. 8, 1943), 660.
12 Warren, *All the King's Men* (New York, Harcourt, Brace & Co., 1946), 462. (All quotations are from this edition.)

For a time, Jack attempts to live out his role as historian, to observe and record disinterestedly the career of "the boss," Willie Stark, but Willie's evil finally impinges upon Jack's life in a very personal way: Willie becomes the lover of Anne Stanton, Jack's childhood sweetheart. And Jack plunges into the "real life" equivalent for historical neutrality—unconsciousness, or as he calls it, the "Great Sleep." For a time he subscribes to the theory of the "Great Twitch," a mechanistic view of life in which man is regarded as an autonomous nervous system. At first he finds it "rather bracing and tonic" because when you believed that, then

> . . . nothing was your fault or anybody's fault, for things are always as they are. And you can go back in good spirits, for you will have learned two very great truths. First, that you cannot lose what you have never had. Second, that you are never guilty of a crime which you did not commit.[13]

Jack's cynicism, however, dissolves in the love and pity he learns to feel for his mother and for his natural father, Judge Irwin. When Willie Stark dies at the hands of Dr. Stanton, Jack is able to see the historical implications of their lives, but at the same time he sees "that though doomed they had nothing to do with any doom under the godhead of the Great Twitch. They were doomed, but they lived in the agony of the will." Willie Stark is the proponent and the embodiment of what Jack calls "the theory of the moral neutrality of history":

> All change costs something. You have to write off the costs against the gain . . . . Process as process is neither morally good nor morally bad. We may judge results not process. The morally bad agent may perform the deed which is good. The morally good agent may perform the deed which is bad. Maybe a man has to sell his soul to get the power to do good.

[13] *Ibid.*, 329–30.

Jack reasons, however, that:

The theory of historical costs. The theory of the moral neutrality of history. All that was a high historical view from a chilly pinnacle. Maybe it took a genius to see it. To really see it. Maybe you had to get chained to the high pinnacle with the buzzards pecking at your liver and lights before you could see it.[14]

Jack Burden at last rejects the theory of the moral neutrality of history and comes to believe that though "History is blind . . . man is not."

In an attempt to explain why so many novelists who are better than Robert Penn Warren have been ignored by the Pulitzer authorities, Arthur Mizener has suggested that Warren has been honored because he shares the conservative views of other Pulitzer novelists.[15] It is true that Warren is conservative, but his conservatism is of a far different stripe. Whereas his predecessors' outlook is primarily social and economic, Warren's is primarily philosophical and moral. Tarkington, Ferber, Bromfield, Barnes, Stribling, Mitchell, Flavin, and the others are concerned mainly with the individual's allegiance to certain rules of conduct having to do with money, work, and sexual behavior; Warren is concerned with the total problem of individual responsibility and the individual conscience. Ironically, the "moral" force in most of the Pulitzer novels is not the individual conscience at all, but the very "historical force" which Warren condemns in *All the King's Men*. For example, it is a historical perspective that allows Margaret Mitchell to exonerate Scarlett O'Hara and Rhett Butler. They are merely acting "out of time," it is

[14] *Ibid.*, 417–18.
[15] Arthur Mizener suggests that Warren belongs on the same side of the moral fence as other Pulitzer novelists: "The Pulitzer Prizes," *Atlantic Monthly*, Vol. CC (July, 1957), 44.

argued, in accord with what later generations will see was necessary for survival. And before sending Martin Arrowsmith off to study the West Indian plague, Dr. Max Gottlieb urges him to take the high historical view from the chilly pinnacle of abstract humanitarianism:

> "You must not be just a good doctor at St. Hubert. You must pity, oh, so much the generation after generation yet to come that you can refuse to let yourself indulge in pity for the men you will see dying."[16]

Although Arrowsmith is not able to maintain that pitiless objectivity and to deny his individual conscience at St. Hubert, he does finally renounce society, wife, and son to go off to a laboratory in the Vermont woods, which Lewis appears to think is a final triumph of the disinterested truth-seeker over the partisan claims of society. Warren, however, holds in *All the King's Men* that "truth" cannot be disinterested and that the pure idealism of Dr. Stanton (cf. Martin Arrowsmith) is incomplete and destructive, and the conclusion of *Arrowsmith* unwittingly confirms this view.

Since *All the King's Men* is an attack on the theory of the moral neutrality of history, to which so many Pulitzer novels are committed, and considering the demonstrated taste of the jurors, it might well be wondered why the authorities voted to give *All the King's Men* a prize. The answer is, doubtless, that the Pulitzer jurors did not recognize the full implications of the novel. For them, as for many of the daily reviewers, *All the King's Men* was probably another historical novel, an account of the "violent regime of Huey Long" for whom Willie Stark seemed but a fictional counterpart.[17] Further, *All the King's Men*, although not a best seller, was

---

[16] Lewis, *Arrowsmith*, 354.
[17] *Book Review Digest* (1946), pp. 858–59.

a fairly popular novel, and though tightly structured and bristling with un-Pulitzer moral, political, and philosophical implications, it employs many of the techniques of popular dramatic forms.

Eric Bentley observed, and Wallace Douglas has since pointed out in detail, Warren's indebtedness to the techniques and stereotypes of the movies.[18] He uses the "close-up," and the "fade-out," the melodramatic gesture, and the external tags by which movie makers indicate "character" on the screen. Jack Burden at times even functions as a kind of neutral camera who merely photographs the scene, as in the following description of Willie Stark's early home:

> It looked like those farmhouses you ride by in the country in the middle of the afternoon, with the chickens under the trees and the dog asleep, and you know the only person in the house is the woman who has finished washing up the dishes and has swept the kitchen and has gone upstairs to lie down for half an hour and has pulled off her dress and kicked off her shoes and is lying there on her back on the bed in the shadowy room with her eyes closed and a strand of her hair still matted down on her forehead with perspiration. She listens to the flies cruising around the room, then she listens to your motor getting big out on the road, then it shrinks off into the distance and she listens to the flies. That was the kind of house it was . . . .[19]

Jack Burden also functions as commentator and interpreter, pointing out philosophical implications and explaining the book's meaning. The last sixteen or so pages constitute, in fact, an explication of the novel, and in this we see an indication of Warren's limitations as a novelist. For although

[18] Eric Bentley, "The Meaning of Robert Penn Warren's Novels," *Forms of Modern Fiction*, ed. by William Van O'Connor (Minneapolis, 1948), 269–86; Wallace W. Douglas, "Drug Store Gothic: The Style of Robert Penn Warren," *College Engl.*, Vol. XV (Feb., 1954), 265–72.
[19] Pages 25–26.

he is an intelligent critic and a writer who is very much in control of his ideas, Warren's characters are sometimes puppets, and his story is an intellectual maze through which the narrator and his author lead the reader in order to reveal what naïve undergraduates call "the hidden meaning." As Eric Bentley puts it, the theme of the novel and its vehicle separate, at last—the vehicle becoming merely an illustration of the theme. Consequently, the implications of Warren's novel rest somewhat less upon his art than upon the explanations provided by Jack Burden's explicit remarks —upon bare statement rather than fictional rendering. Thus, the "narrative voice" of *All the King's Men*, which is handed over to Jack Burden, is the book's chief weakness. Whereas the style of Faulkner, for instance, extends and enriches the meaning of his narrative at almost every point, the style in which *All the King's Men* is written turns back upon the narrator and seems to say, "See how smart, how clever I am?" And although the style may create Jack Burden, "we cannot forgive all the fancy writing, as some critics do, merely on the grounds that the writer is supposed to be Burden and not Warren. Burden was chosen and created by Warren."[20]

In spite of this failure, however, *All the King's Men* is a serious literary work that attempts to view life, not as a simple matter of obeying or breaking rules about money and sex, but as a highly complex tangle of intellectual, moral, emotional, and also very practical considerations. The novel's successes far outweigh its failures, and as was said at the beginning of this section, *All the King's Men* is the best novel ever to be awarded a Pulitzer prize.

[20] Bentley, "The Meaning of Robert Penn Warren's Novels," *Forms of Modern Fiction*, ed. by William Van O'Connor, 285.

CHAPTER SEVEN

World War II as Entertainment and Moral Issue

O N MAY 11, 1947, five days after Robert Penn Warren was given the Pulitzer prize, it was reported in the *New York Times* that the official terms for the Pulitzer novel award had again been changed. In the future, the prize would be given not merely to a "distinguished novel," but to "distinguished fiction in book form": the prize could now be awarded to a collection of short fiction as well as to a novel.[1] Considering that some of the best American fiction written between 1917 and 1947 was in the short story form and that many fine collections of short fiction had been automatically excluded by the old terms, the change was long overdue.

As it turned out, 1947 was as good a year as any for broadening the scope of the fiction award, particularly since a very fine collection of short fiction had been published that year by a promising young writer, *The Prince of Darkness*, by J. F. Powers. It is quite unlikely, however, that Powers' book was seriously considered. For the Advisory Board, it seems, lifted the ban against short story collections only because it wished to give the 1948 award to James A. Michener's *Tales of the South Pacific*. One board member has recently revealed that at the May 1947 meeting, seven months before the close

[1] Page 45.

of the nominating period, some members of the Advisory Board had already made up their minds that *South Pacific* was likely to be the best choice for that year. Thus, when the board reconvened in May of the following year, it must have been somewhat disconcerted to find that the jury of literary experts had not even nominated Michener's book for the prize. Since the Advisory Board had the authority to name the prize-winning work, however, it was a simple matter for it to disregard the jury's recommendation and give the prize to *Tales of the South Pacific*.[2]

Some people might call the award to *South Pacific* a tribute to the Advisory Board's courage and independence, for at the time the prize was given the book was not very widely known. Reminiscing fourteen years later about that decision of the Advisory Board, Arthur Krock remarked that he and the other members of the Board had rescued *South Pacific* from oblivion and set its author on the road to fame and fortune.[3] Since the artistic and intellectual level of *South Pacific* is not much higher than the stage and motion-picture versions of the book, it would be helpful if Arthur Krock had indicated why the Advisory Board went so far out of its way for the book.

The reasons for *South Pacific*'s eventual popularity are not far to seek. In 1947, the war in the Pacific was not long over, and there was still a great deal of interest, among civilians at least, in the delightful details of military life overseas, especially in risqué incidents that made the recent war so human and comical. Michener's book is a lode of this kind of material. Near the end of the book there are accounts of fighting, but most of the emphasis is on the joy of life behind the lines. There are stories about native prostitutes, a roguish

[2] Krock, "In the Nation," *New York Times*, May 11, 1962, p. 30.
[3] *Ibid.*

procuress called Bloody Mary, a nurse from Arkansas who falls in love with a French plantation owner, a jolly fat sergeant called Atabrine Benny because he travels about the islands stuffing the natives with atabrine pills. There is also (to satisfy the "love interest") a detailed account of the affair of Lieutenant Joe Cable and a "delicate Tonkinese" named Liat.

But *South Pacific* has its serious side too. There is a tale about a lone Englishman who spies on the Japanese and, at the risk of his life, broadcasts reports of military activities. There is also some attention paid to a type of wartime villain then popular, a rich snobbish American officer who boasts of his eagerness for battle, but when the chance to fight comes, has himself transferred back to the States. There is also his familiar wartime opposite, the bad boy who makes good. In this case, a daredevil, hard-drinking, non-conformist naval lieutenant who redeems himself at the end of the book by strolling casually into Japanese bullets. There is also a good deal of local color designed to inform the people back home about the fabulous South Seas, some amateur anthropology, and, toward the close of the book, an account of a battle between Japanese and American forces that is told with all of the hairbreadth suspense and thrilling excitement of a war movie or western. Then, in the last chapter, the author turns philosopher to make profound remarks about the meaning of the recent war.

The final scene takes place in a "Cemetery at Hoga Point." As the curtain rises, the narrator is seen leaning against a picket fence feeling "lonely and bitter" about the row upon row of crosses that mark the graves of the 281 Americans who died in the battle of Kuralei, when there shuffles toward him a tall but dignified Negro who begins to deliver shrewd comments about life and death:

Me'n Denis has often remarked dat never again will we be surrounded only by heroes . . . . Dese yeare is de men dat took de las' Jap charge . . . . Wiped out. Ever' one of dem . . . . Some of dem we couldn't even find. Dat is, not all of dem. We jes' had to bury arms and legs and call 'em bodies . . . . But here dey all lie. Sleepin! It doan make no difference to 'em now. Bodies or no bodies. Dey all heroes![4]

It is Commander Hoag's grave, though, about which the Negro is especially solicitous, for although Hoag was a Southerner, he championed the right of "the cullud boys." A "good man," the Negro says of Hoag and then reiterates his simple lament: "Where are we gonna git good men lak him?" The Negro then shuffles upstage, allowing the narrator to take over and deliver his editorial:

I thought of Hoag as I knew him, a man who never buttoned his shirt properly. He was from Atlanta, but he championed the Negro. He was a rich man, but he befriended his meanest enlisted man. He was a gentile, but he placed Jews in position of command. He was a man tired with responsibility, but he saw to it that others got rest . . . . Each man who lay on Hoga Point bore with him to his grave some promise for a free America. Now they were gone. Who would take their places? Women? Old men? Or were those who lived committed to a double burden?[5]

Only by a liberal stretch of one's definition can *Tales of the South Pacific* be called distinguished fiction. It is simply a collection of descriptions, character sketches, unconnected incidents, anecdotes, off-color jokes, patriotic editorials, all loosely held together by a central narrator who can see into the minds of other people and report what is happening in

[4] Michener, *Tales of the South Pacific* (New York, Macmillan Co., 1952), 322. (All quotations are from this edition.)
[5] Page 325.

141

places miles away. Michener's characters are wholly improbable. There is Nellie Forbush, for instance, from Otolousa, Arkansas, who has just about decided not to marry her French suitor because he once "lived with a nigger" (i.e. a South Sea Islander), but who is then jollied out of that prejudice by her friend Dinah who, not being from the South, cannot understand Nellie's feelings. However, all that is needed to reconstruct Nellie is for Dinah to wave an Otolousa newspaper photograph of Nellie labeled "our heroine" several times, and then look at Nellie with tears in her eyes. Nellie then catches a glimpse of herself as she was that afternoon in Otolousa when she told her boy friend, Charlie, that she wouldn't marry him because she wanted to go out and "see the world" and "live with people." Nellie then becomes amused at the "ridiculousness of her situation" and begins laughing at Dinah. Then she laughs at herself. And the "two nurses caught one another by the arms and started dancing." Inadvertently Nellie knocks to the floor the letter she has just written to Charlie, telling him that she will marry him. She picks it up and crumples it into a ball. "So long, Charlie!" she cries, tossing the ball into a corner. And then after a tearful exchange of confidences between the two nurses ("in mutual happiness they blubbered for a while"), and after Dinah "sagaciously" assures Nellie that she will "never have a bored moment around" the Frenchman's daughters, Nellie decides to marry her planter after all.[6]

Since the Advisory Board is made up of newspaper publishers and editors rather than novelists or literary critics, it is not astonishing that they would mistake a bad work of fiction for a good one, but it is somewhat surprising that they should prefer a book that is undistinguished even when judged by the standards of good journalism. Michener's style

[6] Pages 114–15.

is a tasteless mixture of pretentious cant, clichés, and coy vulgarities:

> . . . secure in their mutually shared passions, they surrendered themselves through that night to the reassurances of immortality that men and women can give one another.[7]

The examples of bad writing are almost inexhaustible. In fact, one would be hard-pressed to find a single sentence that could be favorably compared with even the least effective writing in J. F. Powers' *The Prince of Darkness.*

Although we do not know which books the fiction jury recommended for the Pulitzer prize in 1949, it was inevitable that one novel, whether nominated or not, would loom very large in the Pulitzer authorities' consciousness: Norman Mailer's *The Naked and the Dead.* For not only had *Naked and the Dead* been very high on the best seller lists during 1948, but it was also widely discussed by reviewers and popular critics and was said to be one of the most significant novels to come out of the recent war.[8] Though frequently influenced by the size of book sales and the magic of popularity, the Advisory Board was quite capable of ignoring very popular novels. They passed over *Naked and the Dead* and chose, instead, James Gould Cozzens' *Guard of Honor,* which was, as a matter of fact, a moderately good work of fiction.

The setting of *Guard of Honor* is an Air Force base in Florida during the early days of World War II, and all of the major characters are Air Force personnel, including several high-ranking generals. Cozzens' main interests are in the public and private relationships of his characters and in the social, moral, and philosophical implications of these rela-

[7] Pages 179–80.
[8] *Book Review Digest* (1948), pp. 544–45. See especially reviews in *New York Times, New York Herald Tribune, Time,* and *Nation.*

tionships. The most prominent of the public relationships has to do with the conflict between Negroes and whites: a hot-tempered white flyer, Lieutenant Colonel "Bus" Carricker, strikes a Negro pilot in the presence of a number of witnesses, black and white. The Negro officer, Lieutenant Willis, has to be hospitalized, and before the base commander, Major General Beale, can straighten matters out quietly and unofficially, word comes from Washington that Lieutenant Willis has been selected by the Air Force chiefs to receive a decoration for heroic action in Africa. The racial issue is further complicated by the attempt of Lieutenant Willis' fellow Negro officers to force their way into an officers' club that has been declared off-limits to Negroes. News of the assault on Lieutenant Willis and the segregation order, considerably distorted in transmission, is given to Eastern newspapers by a Negro reporter who has been cleared by Washington and aided by Lieutenant Edsell, who is presented by Cozzens as a neurotic white liberal.

Cozzens does not openly take sides in the dispute, but it is quite clear that he agrees with those in the novel who hold that while Negroes are unjustly treated, the wrong way to improve the situation is through forcing the issue. That this is Cozzens' view is supported by the fate of the two Negro officers who lead the assault on the officers' club: they are arrested and threatened with court-martial. In contrast, Lieutenant Willis shows what Cozzens clearly commends as good sense: he refuses to join the rebellious Negro officers and, as payment for persuading his fellow officers to call off their campaign to get into the officer's club, gets a major's commission and command of a new Negro Air Force squadron.

Although the racial issue is the most dramatic element in the novel and though it raises some serious social questions,

Cozzens' ultimate concern is more philosophical than social. The racial conflict, it seems, is important because it is a particular and vivid instance of a more general conservative view, having to do with the relationship of what may be ideal and what is possible. The racial issue, indeed, is seen as just one strand of a complex web of considerations which cannot be dealt with individually or in a social vacuum. For General Beale, the Negro problem is complicated because it is an actual rather than a theoretical problem. In reaching his decision, General Beale has to sort through and assess several conflicting and equally important claims: as Carricker's and Willis' commanding officer, he might be expected to bring formal charges against Carricker for striking a fellow officer. As a friend of Carricker, to whom he owes his life, General Beale feels affection and gratitude. Just prior to striking Lieutenant Willis, Carricker prevented the general's plane from colliding with one piloted by Willis. Indeed, Carricker's attack on Willis was provoked, not by his black skin, but by Willis' pilot error. As a flyer himself and as a high-ranking air force general, Beale is also aware of Carricker's excellence as a pilot and his value to his country's war effort. And so, in his solving of this problem, Beale tries to balance all claims and come to a solution that will work.

Whatever criticisms may be made of Cozzens' position on the Negro issue—and certainly he seems to apologize for segregation—his racial views are not camouflaged by sentimental or pious rhetoric. Whether one likes them or not, they are defended on intellectual grounds that are consistent with and part of a larger conservative concern with how men should face life, if they are to live within the framework of civilized society. In short, Cozzens is honest, as far as he goes.

In *Guard of Honor* there are three ways of meeting life— two extremes and one happy mean: one extreme, best represented by Captain Duchemin, is the way of self-indulgence. Captain Duchemin is preoccupied with little more than sex, whiskey, and food. It is a tribute to Cozzens' art that though the "meaning" of Captain Duchemin comes through clearly, there is nothing moralistic about the way he is presented. He is simply gross, leering, and good-natured, and one reacts to him as one will. At the other extreme is WAC Lieutenant Amanda Turck, who stubbornly clings to an old-fashioned code of chastity even though she begins to feel herself merely prim, even perverted. Toward the end of the novel, Lieutenant Turck succumbs to the somewhat fatherly charms of Captain Nathaniel Hicks, but not before the consumption of a good deal of whiskey, the welling up of unhappy emotions, and the shedding of bitter tears.

Captain Hicks, on the other hand, appears to achieve a kind of ideal balance between these extremes. He does not deliberately seek out sexual experiences: in fact, during much of the novel he remains "loyal" to his wife. But when he does succumb to the "electric touch" of Amanda Turck, he does so without regret and bitter self-recrimination. On a somewhat higher level, General Beale seems to strike a similar kind of balance; though he wavers between conflicting loyalties, when the time to act comes, he gets down from his moral fence and does what the practical man—white or black—must do: he adapts the ideal (in this case, military regulations) to the exigencies of the human situation.

Cozzens' mouthpiece in this novel is Colonel Norman Ross. It is he who sums up most fully the book's philosophical implications. Colonel Ross, in civilian life a lawyer and judge, understands the intellectual problems facing the other characters and discusses them explicitly. About the issue of racial discrimination, he says that it is all very well to have a theory about how life should be lived as long as you don't come up against situations in which the theory cannot be made to work, for "whether you like it or not, there are things you can't buck—no matter how much you want to . . . ."[9] Concerning the colored officers' being denied access to the white officer's club, Colonel Ross tells his wife:

> "In the Air Force, we have now somewhere around three hundred thousand white officers. A certain number of these, I don't know how many, but in relation to the whole, a proportion infinitely larger than that of colored to white officers, an unmanageably large number, hold that a nigger is a nigger. They will not have anything to do with him socially. That is their decision, inculcated in them from their first conscious moments, handed down to them with the sanctions of use and interest. I don't say this couldn't be changed, or that it won't ever be; but it won't today, tomorrow, this week. A man cannot choose to see what he cannot see."[10]

Somewhat earlier in the novel, Colonel Ross puts the matter in more general terms when he says that "rightly called," politics is "the art of the possible"—terms which might well be applied to the view of life taken by most of the sympathetic characters in this novel.[11] One may have ideals and standards which help keep him on the highroad of life, but in the everyday, workaday world, ideals and theories must be trimmed down to permit the work of the real world to be carried on. And the real world includes, besides the chronic drunks, lechers, and incompetents, a great many imperfect individuals given to indulging themselves on occasion in anger, lust, irresponsibility—and these outbursts must be taken for what they are—manifestations of imperfections that do not destroy the usefulness or even the attractiveness

[9] Cozzens, *Guard of Honor* (New York, Harcourt, Brace, 1948), 439. (All quotations are from this edition.)

[10] Page 440.

[11] Page 393.

of the individuals, and this is especially true when the conduct of war, not social amelioration, is the crucial issue. To quote Colonel Ross again:

> A public man had a front, a face; and then, perforce, he had a backside, and in the nature of things it was so ordered that the one was associated with high professions and pronouncements and the other with that euphemistically denoted end-product. They were both always there. Which you saw best would depend on where you stood; but if you let yourself imagine that the one (no matter which) invalidated or made nugatory the other, that was the measure of your simplicity.[12]

And as long as one maintains the proper front in public, the backside can with impunity be permitted to show in private. "All right," says Amanda Turck, agreeing somewhat rigidly to enter the bedroom with Captain Hicks, "but turn out the light."[13]

Until fairly recently the novels of James Gould Cozzens have not been widely read by the general public nor very seriously considered by the critics. But after the publication, in 1957, of *By Love Possessed*, which received fairly wide critical attention and rather impressive sales records, interest in his work quickened. For a time a Cozzens "boom" seemed imminent.[14] Whether or not this interest grows—indeed it appears to be waning already—it is significant to note that the critical battle over Cozzens' fiction has largely raged about the issue of his conservatism.[15] Those who warmly

[12] Page 394.
[13] Page 610.
[14] As of 1958, only six full-length articles on Cozzens had appeared. The most extensive treatment to date is the collection of essays and bibliography in *Critique*, Vol. I (Winter, 1958). There were almost twice as many serious reviews of *By Love Possessed* as there were of *Guard of Honor*. See *Book Review Digest* (1948), p. 180, and *Book Review Digest* (1957), pp. 209–210.
[15] See John Fischer, "The Editor's Easy Chair: Nomination for a

admire his writing seem to feel that at long last a serious and important conservative writer has been given recognition. But to label Cozzens a conservative is merely to beg the question. In some ways (philosophically, morally—perhaps even politically), Faulkner is more conservative than Cozzens. The basic difference between Cozzens and the serious novelists who have dominated American fiction over the past forty-five years is that whereas these writers are critical of the social, political, and moral drift of American life, Cozzens is more or less satisfied with the way things are.[16] Faulkner, Hemingway, Fitzgerald, and even Dos Passos are all, to some extent, idealists. They have a standard of conduct or a code— political, moral, social—against which they measure the world about them. Inevitably they find the world wanting. Cozzens on the contrary, if not exactly complacent, argues that one should take life as it is and do with it what one reasonably can.

For this reason, the relative complexity of Cozzens' style and his philosophic balance somewhat hide a certain moral and psychological superficiality. Cozzens' occasionally involved syntax, his fairly abstract and formal vocabulary, his fluency and urbanity remind one, on occasion at least, of Henry James. But whereas James's style is a means of extracting moral essences from characters and scenes observed from the outside, Cozzens' style, especially when it becomes most highly involved, merely glosses over and makes attractive the surface of things and events. Cozzens is satisfied to

Nobel Prize," *Harper's*, Vol. CCXV (Sept., 1957), 14–15, 18, 20, and John Lydenberg, "Cozzens and the Conservatives," *Critique*, Vol. I (Winter, 1958), 3–9.

[16] John Lydenberg in "Cozzens and the Critics," *College Engl.*, Vol. XIX (Dec. 1957), 99–104 praises this allegiance to the "normal" everyday, responsible world, and condemns the major writers for their sentimental romanticism.

solve the book's specific racial crisis by Lieutenant Willis' compromise and practical attitude, but he does not refer to the larger human issues contained beyond the limited world of military expediency.[17] Cozzens' tendency (it is not quite fatal) to superficiality is difficult to illustrate outside the context of specific scenes, but the following description of one of his best women, Mrs. Ross, makes fairly explicit the nature of his limitations:

> She was a handsome woman—one of those women who, not unattractive when young, still improve with age. Her mature face lost the slight plump softness which never went well with her classically regular features. Her thick, carefully tended hair, now more white than blonde became her. She had been resourceful and competent all her life and the resulting expression of goodtempered firmness suited fifty better than twenty.[18]

There is nothing particularly offensive in this writing, but neither is there any idea, insight, or subtlety expressed here that one might not find, somewhat less smoothly written, in women's magazine fiction.

Expensive jewelry, stylish clothing, high position, and a handsomely preserved exterior are not merely a facade behind which the author probes. For Cozzens' material possessions are an indication that the owner is not only competent in his special field, but that he takes a proper view of success and how it is to be achieved. "You can be sure of getting pretty much what you work for," Nathaniel Hicks, famous editor of a big circulation magazine, thinks. Im-

[17] Walter B. Rideout in a note, "James Gould Cozzens," *Critique*, Vol. I (Winter, 1958), 56, comes to somewhat the same conclusion: "The trouble with [Cozzens] as a writer is not that his personal attitudes are limited, but that they consciously or unconsciously limit his artistic intelligence."

[18] Page 55.

mediately, Captain Hicks questions his truism, and then promptly defends it: "Since when? Since always."[19]

Captain Hicks' platitude calls to mind the sentiments of some earlier Pulitzer prize novels. One thinks of Alice Adams climbing the stairs of Frincke's Business College, and Mr. Lamb riding triumphantly over a Virgil Adams who hasn't the gumption or the talent to produce all of the money he wants. One thinks, too, of Selina DeJong grubbing her millions from the soil, and of Scarlett O'Hara cracking the whip over her convicts; and one envisions too, the Pulitzer heroes and heroines yet to come, bearing within their breasts that simple truth pronounced by Nathaniel Hicks and so dear to the hearts of Pulitzer moralists: you only get what you work for.

Happily, *Guard of Honor* is not wholly platitudinous. Happily, too, it is more skillfully constructed, more tastefully written and more intelligent than Pulitzer novels frequently are. If one had to rank it in the Pulitzer hierarchy, it would come somewhere between Ellen Glasgow's *In This Our Life*, and J. P. Marquand's *The Late George Apley*.[20] After *Guard of Honor*, the Pulitzer authorities took a two-year recess from its fashionable concern with wartime fiction and made a brief retrospective trip back to one of its traditional territories: the frontier. There they found nothing had changed.

Between 1929 and 1942, the Pulitzer jurors had seven excellent opportunities to give a fiction prize to William Faulkner.[21] It is not surprising, of course, that the authorities

[19] Page 358.
[20] Maxwell Geismar places Cozzens in the "rationalist-classicist" tradition of Howells, Edith Wharton, Willa Cather, and Ellen Glasgow. See "By Cozzens Possessed," *Critique*, Vol. I (Winter, 1958), 52.
[21] These are: *The Sound and the Fury* (1929); *As I Lay Dying*

ignored Faulkner's earlier books, for until the early 1940's, his work was largely misunderstood and misrepresented by reviewers and critics. But by the end of the decade, Faulkner's reputation was so well established in this country and in Europe that he was awarded the Nobel prize for literature. In 1949 the Pulitzer authorities might also have honored Faulkner with a Pulitzer fiction prize (for *Intruder in the Dust*) when they instead chose *Guard of Honor*. In the two years immediately after Faulkner won the Nobel award, in 1949, the Pulitzer authorities twice had the opportunity to award him a Pulitzer prize. In 1950 he was eligible with *Knight's Gambit*, and again in 1951 with the *Collected Short Stories*. In both of these years, the authorities gave prizes to two commonplace books about the American frontier. In 1950 they selected *The Way West*, by A. B. Guthrie, Jr., whose best seller, *The Big Sky*, had lost out to *South Pacific* in 1948. In 1951 they selected *The Town*, by Conrad Richter, which was another social history about the settling of the frontier.

The Way West resembles the kind of novel that Pulitzer judges were choosing in the 1920's and 1930's: a loosely constructed narrative about a group of pioneers' migrating in covered wagons from Independence, Missouri, to the Oregon territory. Although there is some attention paid to character development, most of the emphasis is on the hardships of pioneer life: thieving Indians, muddy trails, treacherous fords, scarcity of firewood, rattlesnakes, buffalo stampedes— in short, the stock situations of western adventure stories.

The characters, too, are familiar types from popular frontier mythology. There is Dick Summers, a latter-day

---

(1930); *Light In August* (1932); *Absalom, Absalom!* (1936); *Wild Palms* (1939); *The Hamlet* (1940); and *Go Down, Moses* (1942).

Natty Bumppo, who dresses like an Indian in white buck-skin, leads a wagon train unerringly across the trackless west, speaks with ease the lingo of each Indian tribe encountered, and longs only to recapture the vanished past, which is symbolized for him by a beautiful Indian maiden with whom he once lived on Popo Agie. There, too, is Lije Evans and his wife, a hardy couple who follow worshipfully in the footsteps of Summers until he disappears as the caravan approaches the end of its journey. Summers' passing is to be a symbol, no doubt, of the passing of the old wild West when it was a happy hunting ground for the Indians and for the rare, brave white men like Summers. Guthrie makes clear that Evans and his wife are of the new, less adventurous, but hard-working farming stock who are dutifully serving the forces of historical destiny by being part of the long train of westering pioneers. And, although they suffer all manner of privation, "the thing was worth the cost," Evans concludes, because "no prize came easy . . . . A nation couldn't grow unless somebody dared. The price was high, but who would say it was too high—except for those who'd paid so dear?" As for Summers' dream of the "wild and empty" country of the past—"such things didn't count for much compared with Oregon and the life now opening up. Besides, those times were gone or going."[22]

In dismissing Summers' attachment to the wilderness as fine, but anachronistic, and in holding up the Evanses as the heroes of the newer America, Guthrie joins the ranks of those other Pulitzer historical moralists. For him, it seems that, "what is past is past" is not merely a truism; it is the highest extent to which his moral sense can reach. As Paul Pickerel in the *Yale Review* remarked, *The Way West* is

[22] A. B. Guthrie, Jr., *The Way West* (New York, William Sloane Associates, 1949), 358.

"just another story of western migration."[23] Guthrie's sentimental treatment of the subject, in which characters are merely abstractions seen through the rosy haze of schoolbook history, adds little to one's understanding of either the human experience or the moral and philosophical implications of the western movement generally. Guthrie may have researched his "facts," as some of the reviewers suggested, but he neglects the more important truths which are the serious novelist's proper domain.

With Faulkner's *Collected Stories*, Robert Penn Warren's *World Enough and Time*, and Hemingway's *Across the River and Into the Trees* to choose among, the Pulitzer authorities in 1951 selected another book about the American frontier, *The Town*, by Conrad Richter. Perhaps the most remarkable thing about *The Town* (it was this quality that appealed to the book's most enthusiastic reviewers) is the plethora of historical detail—not just the occasional references to historical personages or events (Johnny Appleseed, Robert Owen, the opening of an Ohio canal)—but the numerous details about the surface of life on the Ohio frontier a hundred or more years ago. The bonnets, dresses, cooking utensils, log cabins, town mansions, lamps, even the jokes and sleeping habits of the pioneer past are scattered through every chapter with such profusion that one feels certain the author meant his book to be taken as a chapter in American social history.

The extent to which Richter has succeeded in evoking the American past for some readers may be judged from the enthusiastic comments of Louis Bromfield (the 1927 novel prize winner), Edward Wagenknecht, and particularly those of J. Donald Adams in his "Speaking of Books" column in the *New York Times*. Mr. Adams was delighted that a Pulitz-

[23] Vol. XXXIX (Winter, 1950), 384.

er prize had been given *The Town* because, among other things, he said, it was "an extraordinary achievement in bringing the past close." Then after quoting with approval a passage in which the chief character, Sayward Wheeler, tells her son to watch for all sorts of newfangled notions for getting out of work, Mr. Adams—carried away by the book's pretensions to historicity—cried, "That was a century ago. And now?"[24]

Although *The Town* somewhat resembles an animated county museum, its main appeal is not simply to the American nostalgia for log cabins and primeval forests. Nor is it merely neutralist history. If *The Town* manages to recreate a sense of the American past, it does so in accordance with the popular myth that the pioneers who chopped down the forests, and cleared the land, and wore buckskin breeches of amazing toughness were—in some mystical way—more moral, more wholesome, and more affectionate than the people who came after them. Men like Worth, father of Sayward, were greater even than Sayward's generation, because they were less "civilized"—(i.e.) they seldom bathed, never stayed in one place very long, or with the same woman, and took a very dim view of those who required more than a "bag of meal" to "feel good." And, of course, the mere fact that Indian blood coursed through the veins of Worth raises his moral stock higher than the whole "civilized" town of Americus and perhaps even of New England.

Sayward, being the daughter of Worth, is also part Indian. She forsakes her cabin in the woods for a fine mansion in town, but it is at the instigation of her husband, a runaway New England aristocrat, too much given to introspection and

[24] *Book Review Digest* (1950), p. 761; *New York Times*, May 20, 1951, p. 2. Adams also said that the trilogy of which *The Town* was the concluding part was "the finest creative achievement we have had on the theme of the westward movement in American life."

free thought (their marriage symbolizes, perhaps, the impact of intellectual New England on the western settlements). Sayward, however, never renounces the old pioneer virtues— hard work, an unadorned face, slicked-back hair, and a "humble rag carpet" on her bedroom floor. Like Selina DeJong, Sayward has all the unpretentiousness of the poor, without the disadvantages of being penniless. And like Selina, too, Sayward is a familiar Pulitzer type, the highly "moral," hard-working individual whose life reads like a homily illustrating how all personal, economic, and social problems can be solved by the proper application of elbow grease. To render his "old-fashioned" political and economic gospel somewhat dramatic, Richter makes Sayward herself his humble spokesman. On one occasion, for instance, when Chancey, Sayward's weak son, advocates the view of Robert Owen, that "if you relieve the people of want, you relieve them of evil and unhappiness," Sayward retorts:

> "Bosh and nonsense, Chancey! . . . Making a body happy by taking away what made him unhappy will never keep him happy long. The more you give him, the more he'll want and the weaker he'll get for not having to scratch for his self. The happiest folks I ever knew were those who raised their own potatoes, corn and garden stuff the first spring out here. They'd have half starved but they found out they could get the best of their own troubles . . . . If making your young ones work off their own troubles is old-fashioned, and out of date, then the good Lord is out of date because that's the way he lets us sink or swim with our troubles.[25]

Just as Sayward Wheeler is obviously a fictional relative of Selina DeJong, Scarlett O'Hara, Cean Carver Smith O'Connor, and those other strong Pulitzer women, so, too, is her son Chancey related to Dirk DeJong, and Ashley

[25] Richter, *The Town* (New York, Alfred A. Knopf, 1950), 311.

Wilkes, and the other weak, young men who want the world on easy or impossibly idealistic terms. As a boy, Chancey dreams, makes up stories, and longs for more refined and sensitive parents. As a young man, he goes in not only for Robert Owen's brand of socialism, but for peace societies and—to the "bamfoozlement" of his mother—writing poems and articles for the newspapers.[26]

If Chancey were a convincing character, one would have to agree that he is a shallow fool who feeds on the empty liberalism of the nineteenth century. But Chancey Wheeler is merely a straw liberal set up in order to be knocked over at the end of the novel, in the name of sentimental conservatism. It may be idiotic to believe that relieving people of hard work will make them happy, but surely this belief is no more simple-minded than venerating the past because men lived in log cabins and did manual labor that they could not avoid doing. It is one thing to find a moral significance in the destruction of the American wilderness—as Faulkner has— and quite another to equate goodness with primitive living, as Richter does. Faulkner is concerned with the moral relationships of his characters to the land and to each other; Richter is concerned with the morality of some practical economic arrangements. The difference between Faulkner and Richter is the difference between a great artist and a copybook moralist.[27]

In 1952 the Pulitzer authorities had another opportunity to give William Faulkner a Pulitzer prize, for *Requiem for a Nun*. Although *Requiem for a Nun* cannot be ranked with Faulkner's earlier and better work, it was certainly a respectable candidate for the 1952 prize, as were William Styron's

[26] Page 312.

[27] See especially Robert Penn Warren, "Cowley's Faulkner," *New Republic*, Vol. CXV (Aug. 12, 1946), 176-80, and (Aug. 26, 1946), 234-37.

Lie down in Darkness, and J. D. Salinger's A *Catcher in the Rye*. But the Pulitzer authorities selected as their "distinguished fiction" for 1952 one of the decade's most popular best sellers, *The Caine Mutiny*, by Herman Wouk.[28]

Like *Tales of the South Pacific*, *The Caine Mutiny* is a blend of popular entertainment and "serious" moralizing. There are two plots: the love story of Willie Keith, youthful scion of a rich Eastern family, and May Wynn (real name Marie Minotti), a poor girl turned night club singer; and the sea story (in which Willie also figures) about life aboard the mine sweeper *Caine*, the "mutiny," and the court martial of the officer who led the mutiny. The sea story ends with the acquittal of the accused officer, and the love story ends with Willie's discovery that May has taken another lover (though she denies having slept with him) and dyed her hair blonde, an action which seems of extraordinary significance to Willie. As the final curtain lowers, May has Willie on tenterhooks: she might marry him and, again, she might not. The story of Willie and May is the stuff out of which soap operas are fashioned. Willie, the spoiled rich boy stereotype popular in World War II songs and motion pictures, is accustomed to being waited on and catered to.[29] He is also a Princeton graduate. Naturally May is beautiful, poor, virtuous, and hard-working. She loves Willie, not, of course, for his money, but for himself. Willie's mother, the "high society" type, naturally dislikes May and tries to keep Willie from marrying

---

[28] As of May 3, 1952, *The Caine Mutiny* was "in its second year on the best-seller list." *Pub. Wkly.*, Vol. CLXI (May 3, 1952), 1871.

[29] I am drawing here on personal recollection. One of the most popular songs of the early war years was "You're in the Army, Mr. Jones," from the Irving Berlin musical *You're in the Army*, which dealt with the beneficial change from a soft life ("breakfast in bed," etc.) to the rigorous, manly routine of the army. Two movies dealing humorously with the same kind of material are: *See Here, Private Hargrove* (also a book) and, *Up in Arms*, starring Danny Kaye, Dinah Shore, *et al.*

her. But at the end of the novel, Willie (matured by his naval experiences) decides to marry May despite his mother's protests and in spite of May's newly dyed hair.

While the "love interest" may have kept some readers entertained, what most intrigued the book's vast audience was Wouk's unorthodox handling of the war material. One of the book's chief characters is a boorish and grossly incompetent sea captain, Philip Francis Queeg. Readers who had been nourished for many years on official wartime propaganda must have been shocked and amused to find that Captain Queeg has none of the dignity or competence traditionally associated with his position as ship's commander. Queeg lounges about the ship naked, or in his underwear. He childishly demands ice cream with maple syrup. He even orders a search of the ship for a non-existent key—all because a few scoops of strawberries are missing from the ship's refrigerator.

In addition to these rather trivial failings, Captain Queeg also manifests a professional incompetence that will probably remain unparalleled in or out of fiction. Queeg frequently breaks naval regulations and even fails to carry out his battle orders. On one occasion, he rams the *Caine* into the side of another ship and then backs it onto a mud band. On another occasion, he cowardly orders his ship to retreat from enemy fire. Throughout three fourths of the novel, Captain Queeg is a thoroughly incompetent and badly frightened man. However, toward the close of the book Wouk springs a wholly unprepared-for surprise: Queeg, he tells us, is not really the incompetent everyone thinks him; he is the victim of ambitious and cowardly subordinates.

In novel form, *The Caine Mutiny* elicited few comments from serious critics. After the story of the mutiny was turned into a successful Broadway show, however, the play version was reviewed by Harold Clurman in the *Nation*, and by Eric Bentley in the *New Republic*.[30] Clurman and Bentley both criticized the play, chiefly for the unwarranted whitewashing of Queeg, and for Wouk's final and rather absurd "message." For all of the *Caine*'s officers observe Queeg's strange behavior and testify to his incompetence. Wouk attempts to whitewash Queeg by blaming the "persecution" of Queeg on the villain of the novel, Lieutenant Tom Keefer. It is Keefer who diagnoses Queeg's neurosis and persuades the ship's executive officer, Lieutenant Maryk, to seize control of the ship during a typhoon when it appears that Queeg is too terrified to issue the orders necessary to save the ship. Maryk is subsequently tried, but through the efforts of Lieutenant Barney Greenwald, his skillful, dedicated, Jewish lawyer, Maryk is acquitted. Later, at a party celebrating Maryk's acquittal, Greenwald appears, slightly drunk, and tells Maryk that it is he, Maryk, not Queeg, who is really guilty of wrongdoing. Indeed, Greenwald suggests that Queeg is something of a hero. Greenwald supports this astonishing assertion by arguing that because Queeg served in the regular Navy when the Nazis were overrunning Europe and killing the Jews, Captain Queeg was "standing guard on this fat dumb and happy country of ours" and keeping American Jews from being murdered, or as Greenwald puts it, "he stopped Hermann Goering from washing his fat behind with my mother."[31]

While it is easy to understand the reason for Lieutenant Greenwald's emotional defense of the United States Navy,

[30] Eric Bentley, "Capt. Bligh's Revenge," *New Republic*, Vol. CXXX (Feb. 15, 1954), 21, and Harold Clurman, "Theater," *Nation*, Vol. CLXXVIII (Feb. 13, 1954), 138.

[31] Wouk, *The Caine Mutiny, A Novel of World War II* (Garden City, New York, Doubleday & Co., Inc., 1954), 446. (All quotations are from this edition.)

it is difficult to see why he—an intelligent trial lawyer, we are told—defends an incompetent American ship's captain who had not served in the Atlantic and who, if he had encountered Nazi warships, would have fled in terror. Greenwald's only defense of Queeg is that he was a member of the regular navy. It would make as much sense to defend a doctor guilty of malpractice on the grounds that he engaged in a humane calling. As Eric Bentley remarks, Wouk's shocking references to Jews' being melted down into soap do not conceal the flaw in Greenwald's defense of Queeg: the war in Europe and Hitler's treatment of the Jews had nothing to do with Queeg's or Maryk's innocence or guilt. It is disturbing to find a Jewish novelist invoking racial stereotypes (inverted ones, to be sure) in this irrational manner.[32]

It is also disturbing to find Wouk employing other kinds of stereotypes: Queeg is recommended to the reader's sympathy in part because his chief critic is an "intellectual" novelist, as Wouk frequently calls Lieutenant Keefer. Certainly there is no reason why an intellectual person should not be the villain of a novel any more than, say, a business man or a lawyer—provided, of course, that the villain's villainy is convincingly particularized. Lieutenant Keefer, however, is likely to convince only those for whom "intellectual" is a term of derision, and for whom serious literature and Freudian psychology are painfully unenlightening. Wouk's readers are invited to identify themselves with Lieutenant Maryk, a gullible "good guy" who made a straight C-minus in college and who, by his own admission, is a "dumb comic-book reader."[33] Another aspect of Wouk's anti-intellectual-

[32] A number of reviewers complained of this sudden, unprepared for reversal. See John Mason Brown, "Operation Bligh," *Sat. Rev.*, Vol. XXXVII (Feb. 6, 1954), 24; *Book Review Digest* (1951), pp. 971–72; and Bentley, "Capt. Bligh's Revenge," *New Republic*, Vol. CXXX (Feb. 15, 1954), 21.
[33] Page 446.

ism is bound up with his use of the word "sensitive," especially in relation to Keefer. Usually "sensitive" is combined with "novelist," and Keefer is presented with heavy-footed irony as a man who pretends to great sensitivity but "tears down" other people, and who writes obscene books in order to make money. Wouk never provides any samples of Keefer's fiction, but we are told that his writing resembles the work of all of those other "sensitive" novelists whom Wouk finds offensive—Proust, Dos Passos, Joyce, Hemingway, and Faulkner.[34]

However, Wouk does not rely entirely on name-calling to blacken his villain. Toward the end of the novel, he arranges matters so as to "prove" that Keefer is a bigger coward even than Queeg. During Maryk's court martial, Keefer betrays his friends and denies that he has ever thought Queeg insane. To make certain that readers react properly to this denial, Wouk later has Barney Greenwald charge Keefer with cowardice and hurl a glass of *yellow* wine in his face.[35] Then, to make absolutely certain that the reader gets the point, Wouk puts the *Caine* under Keefer's command and lets us see how Keefer behaves. And, of course, novelist Keefer does very badly. When a mine bobs up under the ship's prow, Wouk tells us that Keefer squeaks with excitement. His eyeballs even take on an "opaque yellowish look and are rimmed with red." Whenever Keefer gets the opportunity he retires "into an isolation like Queeg's—except that he [works] on his novel instead of solving jigsaw puzzles."[36] Finally Keefer surpasses even Queeg in cowardice by committing the most heinous of all naval crimes: he abandons the ship before it sinks. To make Keefer's cowardice even

[34] Page 268.
[35] Page 468.
[36] Page 450.

more obvious, Wouk arranges matters so that the ship does not sink and Captain Keefer is made to seem ridiculous as well as contemptible.[37]

Artistically and intellectually, *The Caine Mutiny* ranks somewhere between *Gone With the Wind* and *Journey in the Dark*. And like those two novels, it combines entertainment with "serious" moralizing about American life. The story of Willie Keith's transformation from a spoiled rich boy to a mature sea captain (Willie finally becomes commander of the *Caine*) is, like *Journey in the Dark*, intended as an allegory of America's own "coming of age" during World War II. For this we have no lesser authority than Willie's father, who says, in one of several long letters by means of which Wouk sometimes inserts information into his narrative:

> ... Willie. It seems to me that you're very much like our whole country—naive, spoiled and softened by abundance and good luck, but with an interior hardness that comes from your sound stock. This country of ours consists of pioneers, after all, these new Poles and Italians and Jews as well as the older stock, people who had the gumption to get up and go and make themselves better lives in the new world.[38]

Thus, Willie Keith it seems, must be added to the company of Pulitzer prize heroes who succeed through "gumption" and "get up and go," without the aid of family money or prestige, though for Willie the money is nice to come home to after the war. There is, however, a significant difference between the nature of Willie's success and that of his predecessors. Willie's (and America's) maturity consists of a willingness blindly to follow authority wherever it may lead. This is what the conclusion of *The Caine Mutiny*

[37] Pages 451–55.
[38] Page 60.

implies: the orders of an incompetent, perhaps even an insane leader should be obeyed, even though the ship sinks and all hands are lost. *The Caine Mutiny*, interestingly, has been cited by William H. Whyte, Jr. as evidence of a shift that has taken place in popular American morality, from a belief in the integrity of the individual to a bland acceptance of the obligation of the individual to adjust to "the system," whatever its faults, and to incompetents, like Queeg, who stand in positions of appointed authority.[39]

One wonders how the author of *The Caine Mutiny* would reconcile this apparent belief in individual adherence to appointive authority with his obvious disapproval of the Nazis' abuse of authority. One wonders, too, how the Pulitzer authorities would square such a belief with their usual preference in the past for books that preached the gospel of individualism.

[39] William H. Whyte, Jr., *The Organization Man* (New York, 1956), 243–48. Also, see especially Willie's letter to May, page 468, *The Caine Mutiny*.

CHAPTER EIGHT

C*elebrities and Best Sellers*

THE DECISIONS of the Pulitzer authorities during the next five years, from 1953 through 1957, were again fairly typical of past performances, not so much because the themes and subject matters of the prize books were trite or obvious, nor because the artistic level was uniformly low, but because these awards reflected the authorities' habit of avoiding the best fiction of the period. They chose to honor novelists who were famous men of letters or popular best-selling authors (or both), and ignored the work of the not so well-known highly gifted younger writers. During this period both Hemingway and Faulkner were finally given Pulitzer prizes, but for books that were much inferior to their earlier work. MacKinlay Kantor, a fairly prolific best-selling author most widely known perhaps for *The Voice of Bugle Ann*, was awarded the 1956 prize for *Andersonville*, a work about the Andersonville Civil War prison camp. In 1957 Kenneth Roberts, who had produced some half a dozen books of historical fiction over a twenty-seven year period, was given a special citation because "his historical novels . . . have long contributed to the creation of great interest in our early American history."[1]

During this same period, the Pulitzer judges overlooked

[1] *New York Times*, May 7, 1957, p. 29.

the books of a talented but relatively unknown group of writers. *Invisible Man*, by Ralph Ellison, and *Wise Blood*, by Flannery O'Connor, were both eligible in 1953 when the prize went to Hemingway's *The Old Man and the Sea*. J. D. Salinger's *Nine Stories*, Jean Stafford's *Children Are Bored on Sunday*, and Saul Bellow's *The Adventures of Augie March* were all available in 1954 when the authorities refused to give an award on the grounds that "the year 1953 had produced no novel by an American author that merited such distinction."[2]

By 1953 a prize to Ernest Hemingway was long overdue. It was not surprising, of course, that the judges who voted awards to *Alice Adams* and *So Big* did not consider *The Sun Also Rises* as a suitable contender for the 1927 prize—which went to *Early Autumn*, Louis Bromfield's pale Gothic horror. But by 1930, when *A Farewell to Arms* was eligible, it should have been evident even to the Pulitzer judges that although Hemingway sinned against Victorian manners and morals, he was an important, even a respected novelist. With the passing of years and as Hemingway's public life was glamourized in newspaper and picture magazines, he began to accumulate an aura of celebrity that in this country is ordinarily reserved for movie stars and baseball players. He was widely photographed, quoted, and written about. A number of his novels and short stories were also converted into financially successful motion pictures.[3] In 1941 Hemingway's most talked-about and popular novel, *For Whom the Bell Tolls*, was nominated for the Pulitzer prize by the Advisory Board,

[2] *Ibid.*, and May 4, 1954, p. 1.

[3] Between January, 1929, and June, 1941, articles about and photographs of Hemingway appeared in such diverse publications as *Christian Century*, *American Mercury*, *Newsweek*, *Time*, *Life*, *Saturday Review*, *Business Week*, *Fortune*, *New Republic*, *Canadian Forum*, *Scholastic*, *American Review*, *Atlantic Monthly*, and *Commonweal*.

but through the intervention of Nicholas Murray Butler it failed to get the prize.[4] In 1953, however, Hemingway's fiction had at last become sufficiently wholesome and morally edifying. *The Old Man and the Sea*, which was less controversial even than *Laughing Boy* (1930), and a good deal more popular, won the 1953 Pulitzer fiction prize.[5]

The Old Man and the Sea did not sell as well in book form as had *For Whom the Bell Tolls*, which led the best seller lists in 1940, but it had appeared in *Life* magazine and was read, presumably, by millions of people who ordinarily do not read novels.[6] It also enjoyed a popular critical success, as the *Saturday Review* discovered through its annual poll of book reviewers: *The Old Man and the Sea* was the overwhelming choice of all the book reviewers who had been queried. Steinbeck's *East of Eden* was a poor second, and Ralph Ellison's *Invisible Man* received only one vote, cast by Alfred Kazin.[7]

In some ways, *The Old Man and the Sea* resembles Hemingway's earliest work. There is some of the same tersely mannered prose to be found in the stories collected in *In Our Time*; there is a primitive hero, Santiago, who resembles some of the early "code heroes" (like Manuel of "The Undefeated"); and there is a fishing experience that recalls the "tragic adventure" of "The Big Two-Hearted River." Despite these similarities to Hemingway's early work, however, *The Old Man and the Sea* clearly belongs to his later, decadent phase. For although Santiago conforms to the usual Hemingway pattern, he is significantly different from those unflinch-

---

[4] Krock, "In the Nation," *New York Times*, May 11, 1962, p. 30.
[5] Though on the best seller list for about five months, it never reached first place as did *For Whom the Bell Tolls. Pub. Wkly.*, Vol. CLXII (Oct.–Dec., 1952), and Vol. CLXIII (Jan.–May, 1953).
[6] Vol. XXXVI, May 16, 1953.
[7] *Sat. Rev.*, Vol. XXXVI (May 16, 1953), 21.

ing men who face death and defeat determined to make a good show of it. Santiago is defeated, but unlike Jake Barnes, or Frederick Henry, and the other proud losers, he accepts his defeat humbly and without bitterness, plucking from it the simple but saving observation that it is not life that has defeated him, not "they" who have caught him off base as they had Catherine and Frederick; it is, Santiago says, "nothing" that has beat him. "I went out too far."[8]

And unlike his predecessors, Santiago also enjoys a kind of sentimental rescue from defeat. The morning after he returns with the skeleton of the great marlin that he has caught, he is visited by the boy who has fished with him and who had deserted his beloved "old man" only because he is ordered to do so by his own father. "The boy saw that the old man was breathing and then he saw the old man's hands and started to cry." The boy gets the old man some coffee and brings it to him, forces him to drink, and then cheers him up. Now then, he says, we will "fish together again."[9] The novel ends with the old man asleep, dreaming of lions as the boy watches over him.

There had always been a strong undercurrent of sentimentality in Hemingway's writing, though in his best work he managed to control it—partly by means of a tight-lipped narrative style and the frequent use of understatement. In *The Old Man and the Sea*, however, the sentimentality breaks through not only at the end of the book but in a number of passages throughout the novel. Most conspicuous are those places where Santiago is made to think of the stars as his brothers, and to identify himself with the moon, sun, and ocean because they all must sleep. We are even told that

[8] Hemingway, *The Old Man and the Sea* (New York, Charles Scribner's Sons, 1952), 138. (All quotations are from this edition.)
[9] Pages 134, 139.

168

Santiago is very fond of flying fishes as they were his "principal friends on the ocean."[10]

To argue, as some critics do, that as a primitive person, Santiago might be expected to make such anthropomorphic identifications, is beside the point.[11] The language by means of which this identification is made is not Santiago's. It is Hemingway's. This is not mere quibbling. In Hemingway's earlier work, the narrative voice and the sensibility of the chief characters are so closely related that one feels the language and perceptions are those of the character. In *The Old Man and the Sea*, one occasionally feels the fusion of the narrative voice with the mind of Santiago, but more often one is made aware of the presence of the author, editorializing, sentimentalizing, and insisting on his meaning. For example, when the sharks approach Santiago's boat, drawn by the blood of the giant marlin that Santiago has heroically caught, and which the sharks will fiercely devour, Hemingway has his hero cry, "Ay," and then he explains:

> There is no translation for this word and perhaps it is just a noise such as a man might make, involuntarily, feeling the nail go through his hands into the wood.[12]

In an ordinary novelist one might forgive an occasional sentence like this, which so baldly states what, if it is to be convincing, can only be evoked, but in a novelist of Hemingway's achievement such creaky rhetoric is difficult to forgive. Reading it, one is reminded of the great stories of the early Hemingway ("The Killers," "The Undefeated," etc.) in which not a sentence—not even a word—rings false.[13] Clearly, *The*

[10] Pages 32, 85.
[11] I have often heard this defense made in discussions, although I have never seen it in print.
[12] Page 107.
[13] Critics and reviewers have commented on the forced symbolism of this novel. See especially Nemi D'Agostino, "The Later Hemingway (1956),"

Old Man and the Sea is the work of a talented writer in decline, "a monument serving to remind us of earlier glories."[14]

In 1955, six years after he was presented with the Nobel prize in literature, William Faulkner was awarded the Pulitzer fiction prize for his nineteenth work of fiction. In some ways, *A Fable* is Faulkner's most ambitious novel. It was nine years in the making and was meant to be—or at least the publishers hoped it would be—"one of the most notable contributions to American letters in our time."[15] And certainly Faulkner reached far beyond his usual regional material for a subject that has nothing to do, on the surface at least, with the South or with Faulkner's mythical Yoknapatawpha County. The locale is France during World War I; the characters are, for the most part, French; the theme has to do with War, Love, Hate, Compassion, Redemption, and other concepts only implicit in his earlier work.

The central episode of the novel, to which all the characters and minor events are related, concerns the mutiny of a division of French soldiers who are ordered to attack an opposing division of Germans, and then the apprehension, trial, and execution of the French corporal who inspires three thousand soldiers to lay down their arms. This single event produces national and international repercussions that directly involve French, English, Germans, and Americans, including: principally, the commander of the French division that mutinies; the corps commander; the marshal who

---

trans. by Barbara Melchiori Arnett, *Sewanee Rev.*, Vol. LXVIII (Summer, 1960), 482–93; Mark Schorer, "With Grace Under Pressure," *New Republic*, Vol. CXXVII (Oct. 6, 1952), 19–20.

[14] Robert P. Weeks, "Fakery in *The Old Man and the Sea*," *College Engl.*, Vol. XXIV (Dec., 1962), 192.

[15] A statement made in the dust jacket blurb.

commands all the French forces as well as those of the British and Americans fighting in France; a German general; a British flyer; a cockney groom; a horse racer and gambler; an American Negro preacher, and his grandson; the French corporal's band of twelve apostles; and the three women who follow the French corporal—his sister, sister-mother, and "wife."

Unlike many of Faulkner's books, which appear to have been written at top speed, A *Fable* gives evidence of having been carefully—too carefully—worked out. The events of the novel are deliberately constructed so as to follow the events of Passion Week—the apprehension, imprisonment, trial, crucifixion, and resurrection of Christ. And a number of Faulkner's characters are deliberately modeled on figures from Christian tradition: the corporal is a modern representation of Christ; the three women—Marya, Marthe, and the woman called "the whore," clearly represent the mother, sister, and the prostitute who followed Christ to the cross and afterward claimed his body. The corporal's twelve followers are rather obviously meant to suggest Christ's twelve disciples.

A further indication of the kind of planning that went into this novel is Faulkner's handling of the military men. The generals in A *Fable* are all devoted to their profession, but each is moved by different considerations. The general of the division, Charles Gragnon, is concerned mainly with his simple code of "daring, without fear or qualm or regret," and when his troops desert in battle, he resolutely and steadfastly demands the death sentence for all three thousand of them. Next in Faulkner's military hierarchy is General Lallemont, the corps commander, who speaks in a voice "harsh and strong" of the opportunity "to lie some day in the casket of a general or a marshal among the flags of our nation's glory in the palace of the Invalides—".[16] It is "man who is our enemy," says General Lallemont, "the vast seething moiling spiritless mass of him" which only once in a lifetime and then only by means of a great general "with the stature of a giant" can be heaped, and pounded, and stiffened purposeful for a time, until the mass discoheres "faster and faster flowing and seeking back to its own base anonymity."[17]

At the very top of Faulkner's military hierarchy stands the "great general," a man "with the stature of a giant," who commands all the allied forces and who is called by Faulkner only "the marshal" or "the old general." He not only molds men into a purposeful mass for the fighting of wars, but he also understands man's capacity for endurance and expresses himself in a gorgeous rhetoric reminiscent of Faulkner's acceptance speech for the Nobel prize:

> "Oh, yes, [man] will survive it because he has that in him which will endure even beyond the ultimate worthless tideless rock freezing slowly in the last red and heatless sunset, because already the next star in the blue immensity of space will be already clamorous with the uproar of his debarkation, his puny and inexhaustible voice still talking, still planning; and there too after the last ding dong of doom has rung and died there will still be one sound more; his voice, planning still to build something higher, faster, louder . . . .[18]

Faulkner, of course, does not accept the marshal's vision of man as final, just as he did not do so in his Nobel prize speech. It is not merely man's voice that will endure, but his soul and what Faulkner means by *soul* is made clearer by the words of the corporal and by the conclusion of the novel.

[16] Faulkner, A *Fable* (New York, Random House, 1954), 29. (All quotations are from this edition.)
[17] Page 30.
[18] Page 354.

Shortly before his execution, the corporal is taken from his prison cell by the old general, driven into the hills outside Paris and offered his freedom. Nothing, says the general, neither power, glory, wealth, pleasure, or even freedom from pain "is as valuable as simple breathing, simply being alive . . . ."[19] And he offers the corporal his life—the use of his staff car and clearance to the coast, where a ship will take him from the country. But the corporal refuses the marshal's temptation because even though the three thousand soldiers have already deserted him (as the marshal points out), there is still the band of ten or so men who continue to believe and to follow. And so the corporal allows himself to be executed rather than renounce, by fleeing, his beliefs.

The meaning of the corporal's act is made clear by a brief scene at the close of the novel. The corporal has been dead four years when there suddenly appears at his farm, now run by his sisters, a horribly maimed British veteran who is making a kind of pilgrimage to the corporal's home. The same veteran reappears in Paris just as the cortege of the great marshal, now dead, halts before the *Arc de triomphe* and the Tomb of the Unknown Soldier. Amidst the throngs of French patriots gathered to pay homage to their dead hero, the maimed Britisher flings down the medal awarded him by the French government, crying: "Listen to me, too Marshal! This is yours: take it . . . . You too helped carry the torch of man into that twilight where he shall be no more; these are his epitaphs: They shall not pass. My country right or wrong. Here is a spot which is forever England—"[20]

Before he can finish what he has to say, the crowd of loyal patriots leaps upon him and bears him down. As he lies unconscious, a small circle of people surround him, including

[19] Page 350.
[20] This and the following quotations are from A *Fable*, pp. 436–37.

173

THE PULITZER PRIZE NOVELS

the police who have rescued him. "We know him," one of the policemen says, "An Englishman. We've had trouble with him ever since the war; this is not the first time he has insulted our country and disgraced his own."

"Maybe he will die this time," another voice says.

Just then the wounded man opens his eyes, coughs and turns his head. An old man "with a vast worn sick face with hungry and passionate eyes above a white military moustache" appears and holds up the Englishman's head so that he can spit out the blood and the shattered teeth. Then he looks up at the ring of faces and laughs.

"That's right," he says. "Tremble, I'm not going to die. Never."

"I'm not laughing," the old man says. "What you see are tears."

This concluding scene dramatizes the main point of the novel: that man and his folly will not only endure, but, as the marshal says, "they will prevail." Also, as the corporal implies and as the maimed veteran demonstrates, the virtues of pity, compassion, and sacrifice will never be entirely destroyed as long as there is even one believer capable of making the sacrifice that can arouse these emotions.

Though critical opinion has not yet solidified and there appears to be some difference of opinion as to whether A Fable is a very great or a very bad novel, I must agree with Allen Tate's judgment that A Fable is William Faulkner's one bad book.[21] And it is tempting to make much of the fact that this novel more nearly resembles other Pulitzer prize winners than it does Faulkner's earlier work. It is allegory rather than fiction. Characters and setting are fashioned only so as to illustrate the author's thesis, and there is not the

21 "William Faulkner, 1897–1962," *Sewanee Rev.*, Vol. LXXI (Winter, 1963), 161.

usual solidity of specification found in Faulkner's best fiction. The corporal, for instance, who is said to have persuaded three thousand soldiers to mutiny, is not presented directly until the end of the book, and his supposed power over men's hearts is never convincingly demonstrated. Ideas put into the mouths of characters are too often explicit statements of ideas that were implicit in earlier works dealing with Southern material, which is therefore deeply rooted in social, economic, and political institutions, and a way of life convincingly rendered. A *Fable* is interesting mainly because of the light it sheds on Faulkner's ideas, which are less baldly and also more interestingly and convincingly set down in other novels.

In 1956, after the awards to Hemingway and Faulkner for books which were inferior performances (although they are among the half a dozen or so more sound decisions in the forty-five years of prize-giving), the Pulitzer authorities re-asserted their usual preference for commercially successful, popular fiction. They by-passed Flannery O'Connor's brilliant collection of short stories, *A Good Man is Hard to Find*, and selected *Andersonville*, by MacKinlay Kantor.

Andersonville is a sprawling book (768 pages, including a map, bibliography, and biography of the author) about the Andersonville Civil War prison camp in central Georgia, where thousands of Union soldiers died of disease, exposure, and malnutrition. Having neither plot nor theme, the book is composed of fairly long expository accounts of the lives and adventures of various prisoners. There are also several chapters dealing with a neighborhood squire, Ira Claffey, his daughter Lucy, and the man Lucy finally marries, a youngish Confederate army surgeon. A good deal of space is allotted to the everyday, humdrum lives of the Claffeys and their slaves, their manner of planting carrots, dying cloth, making "nectar," playing parlor games, and other such things. Also, a number of chapters and chapter sections are given over to describing the sordid antics of Widow Tebbs, a feeble-minded prostitute whom the author presents in a manner reminiscent of Erskine Caldwell. Perhaps, as Henry Steel Commager suggested in his review of this book, Widow Tebbs and her offspring are intended as "comic relief" from the long and very detailed descriptions of the prisoners and their monotonous life in the stockade.[22]

Kantor's main interest appears to be in describing the horrors of the Andersonville prison. The ragged, threadbare prisoners, the revolting and poisonous food, the unsanitary conditions, the deaths from disease, starvation, shooting, beating and hanging administered by the prisoners them-selves—all of these and many other equally sordid details fill page after page, chapter after chapter. If it is Kantor's aim to convince the reader of the horrors of Andersonville prison, it must be said that he overshoots his mark. For the final effect of all this emphasis on blood, pus, rotting corpses, vomit, diarrhea, and gangrene is to disgust rather than to horrify. That is, the reader's disgust is due less to the atrocities and the sufferings than it is to the author's tasteless and vulgar style. Eric Torrosian, a prisoner who tries to es-cape from the stockade by playing dead, is carried off and thrown onto a pile of rotting corpses that smell

> . . . like a dog run over by a beer wagon . . . rotting even before the rot of unliving flesh began. . . . like . . . the reek of privies and corruption found in oozing drainpipes, they were the garbage box, the neglected fallen greasy flakes in gutters of fish markets and left in the sun . . . old vomit, old bandages, old pus. . . . their tongues were thrust out sometimes, the fluid ran

22 "A Novel of an Infamous Prison in the Civil War," *New York Times*, Oct. 30, 1955, pp. 1, 32.

from their mouths sometimes, the fluid ran from other orifices of their bodies sometimes . . . .[23]

The appeal to "realism" is here made only for the sake of shock.

On the other hand, in the chapters dealing with the genteel white Southerners, Kantor's language becomes absurdly pretentious—as, for example, when Ira Claffey muses about the building of the Andersonville prison camp:

> What ugliness—to know that there would soon be a prison adjacent to one's dooryard! He supposed that prisons were necessary, but the thought of this stockade pained him even before it was made. He counseled himself that he should be glad there was a prison—and in such a healthy area as this— for a prison meant that the young fellows who'd be placed in it were living still; they were not extinct as the Claffey boys were extinct, but they were breathing and able to walk around, even restrained by the fence of massacred pine trees. If there were no places of military detention it would mean that every individual who yielded to superior force was slaughtered when he yielded.[24]

These words are, of course, merely a discursive presentation of what is supposed to be an emotional response.

Kantor's attempts to create characters are quite as unconvincing as his style. He merely writes, for instance, that Lucy, Ira's daughter, is entertaining erotic thoughts about Captain Harry Elkins. And then at the end of the novel, when he wishes to bring Lucy and Harry Elkins together in that embrace which, it seems, is the inevitable climax of popular novels about the Civil War (even one as unpretty as this), his attempt to provide motivation is hilariously inept.

[23] Kantor, *Andersonville* (Cleveland and New York, The World Pub. Co., 1955), 250. (All quotations are from this edition.)
[24] Page 58.

Throughout most of the novel, Harry resists the advances of Miss Lucy, who on one occasion rushes up and plants a kiss on Harry's mouth. Very "rudely," Harry pushes Lucy away and mumbles: "No, no . . . I can't bear it. We can't—Not in this! There's so much filth and screaming. You should hear the gangrenous!" For several hundred more pages, Harry resists Lucy's charms. Then, just before the arrival of the Yankees, Harry suddenly succumbs to Lucy's beauty. Why? Because, Kantor writes, they were all "alone, sole alone, alone in the house, alone and unwatched and unguarded." And also, "there suddenly shafted an enormous desire." But why, the author persists in his questioning, should "stockade and hospital diminish into oblivion now," when they "refused to diminish before?" The answer simply is "weariness": "Weariness gave desperation, desperation gave strength" and almost before either one knew what was happening, Harry (whose "grating laugh" and "great balding squirrel-like head" gave Lucy a "strange" joy) whirls Lucy against him and smothers her mouth with his, while the candle and the crockery on the table are upset and go smash amidst the "faintest smell" of ham "newly scorched."[25]

Finally, the novel's "moral" is quite as pat, clichéd, and unreal as the style and characterization. Ira Claffey, the only character who could be called the hero of the novel, supports the Confederacy as any patriotic Southerner must, sacrificing both sons and worldly goods, but when the end of the war comes and the South is defeated, he finds his "philosophy in history," telling himself that the institution of slavery is evil because it has perished. Although "for his own part he saw little difference between a legal slavery and an economic one," he feels that the Negroes who had been his slaves were better off than the "sickly whites" who worked in Northern mills.

[25] Pages 487, 635.

And so, Ira accepts the fact that a new nation has been made, even though he prayed not to see it, and that there now exists some mystical bond that links his plantation with the land of Maine and Texas and Oregon:

> Because granule of soil lay next to granule of soil and small roots were intertwined, and fences broke down in one patch of woods but rose in the next; and rivers were not bottomless, there were earth and rocks underneath, the rocks touched, it was the land, it was all the American land and the American waters belonging principally to America and not to individual planters, and not to New York or Georgia, as had been so cruelly demonstrated.[26]

Neither the mitigated horrors of slavery, nor the highly dramatized horror of the prison camp are allowed to have any effect as the book ends. The result is the same as if a novel called *Dachau* were concluded with the embrace of young lovers and the statement, "well that's over and done with, and all's well that end's well." This discrepancy between the narrator's dependence on shock and horror and the sugary, evil-is-washed-away-with-a-virgin's-kiss ending is perhaps the most disgusting aspect of an incredibly disgusting novel.

No official reasons, other than the usual announcement that *Andersonville* was "distinguished fiction," were given for its selection. But the comments made in the columns of the *New York Times*, although not attributed to the Pulitzer officials, have the ring of official prose. "Besides effective story telling," it was said, "Mr. Kantor has achieved realism and authenticity by prefacing his writing with solid sessions of research, close study of his territory and old records."[27] It could be that the newspaper editors and publishers (or whoever assisted the Advisory Board in making its decision) were

26 Page 762.
27 *New York Times*, Oct. 30, 1955, p. 32.

impressed by the extensive bibliography and the Anderson-ville map appended to the novel. Perhaps they were also in-fluenced by Kantor's assertion that several characters "are of history and are not invented," and the even more curious remark that the rest of the characters "are drawn from life to the best of the author's ability; and in his most earnest opinion, are portraits of individuals who did exist and con-tribute of their lives to this moment in history."

Whether *Andersonville* is soundly based on fact or not is beside the point, of course. It is a novel, and as such is an interpretation of life, not a history of the Civil War, and it must be judged accordingly. As a novel, it is most undistinguished:

> *Andersonville* is a historical novel, roughly the size of a sand-bag, that retells in wet, straining prose, the story of Anderson-ville prison . . . . Mr. Kantor was apparently fascinated by the monstrousness of his subject, a feeling he transmits to the reader with excruciating care.[28]

28 *New Yorker*, Vol. XXXI (Oct. 29, 1955), 163.

CHAPTER NINE

Continuation of the Great Tradition

W ITH THE EXCEPTION of the award to James Agee's A *Death in the Family*, the next five decisions of the Pulitzer authorities—the last to be treated in this study—do nothing to contravene the general trends established during the first forty years of the Pulitzer novel prize. The books of the most gifted writers of the period, notably Flannery O'Connor, Philip Roth, J. D. Salinger, and John Updike, were ignored and the prizes given to best-selling popular fiction. In both subject matter and in literary quality these most recent prize winners resemble the novels to which Pulitzer awards were often given in the 1920's and 1930's, though they are somewhat more skillfully (i.e., slickly) written.

In A *Death in the Family*, James Agee is concerned for the most part with the accidental death of Jay Follet, a young husband and father, and the effect of his dying on his wife and children. The best qualities of the book are the sensitive and precise language, the specific details which bring scenes and characters alive, and the sharp insights into the minds and feelings of the major characters. It would be very easy in a novel dealing with such a stock—domestic disaster to slip into bathos, but Agee doesn't fake, and he makes few appeals to formula responses or to the mawkishness often found in Pulitzer fiction.

A less honest writer, for instance, might have sentimentalized the son's reactions to his father's death by eliminating any "unworthy" thoughts and feelings, and by exaggerating the boy's sense of loss. But Agee shows the boy, Rufus, on the morning after the father's death as he eagerly discusses with his schoolmates the details of his father's accident and uses the occasion to make himself look important. It is only later when Rufus sees his father in the coffin that the full import of the word *dead* sinks in:

> . . . he turned his eyes from the hand and looked toward his father's face and, seeing the blue-dented chin thrust upward, and the way the flesh was sunken behind the bones of the jaw first recognized in its specific weight the word *dead*.[1]

Also among Agee's most impressive achievements in his sensitive evocation of specific places and people: Knoxville in 1915; Rufus and his Aunt Hannah shopping; the ancient grandeur of the Follet's great-great grandmother; the patient waiting of Mary Follet for the news of her husband's accident. All of these scenes and characters are evoked with a clarity and effectiveness which, in turn, make possible another of Agee's triumphs. As Dwight Macdonald has pointed out, Agee skillfully and successfully dramatizes "domestic love," a subject ordinarily reserved to the women's magazines.[2] The emotions depicted are ordinary and quiet, yet at the same time, one feels, genuine. For these reasons, among others, *A Death in the Family* is convincing in a way few of the Pulitzer novels are.

However, in spite of its superiority to the kind of fiction

[1] Agee, A *Death in the Family* (New York, McDowell, Obolensky, 1957), 311. (All quotations are from this edition.)
[2] Dwight Macdonald, "Death of a Poet," *New Yorker*, Vol. XXXIII (Nov. 16, 1957), 224.

commonly awarded the Pulitzer prize, *A Death in the Family* is not without its flaws, some of which are more serious than the book's enthusiastic admirers have recognized.[3] In the first place, the novel was unfinished at the time of the author's death and was put in publishable form by its editors. And, although there are assurances that the book is presented "exactly" as Agee wrote it, several large sections (about seventy pages) were arbitrarily inserted by the editors.[4] Consequently, no final appraisal of the novel can be made— unless the uncertainties about the form can be removed. The critic's task is further complicated by the presence in these interpolated passages of some sentimental, imprecise, and falsely poetic language. In the section that begins: "Waking in the darkness," for instance, there are sentences that do little more than communicate a vague feeling about the experience the author is attempting to create. A good sample is the disquieting, sentimental apostrophe that Agee puts in the mouth of a little boy:

> My darkness. Do you listen? Oh, are you hollowed, all one taking ear?
> My darkness. Do you watch me? Oh, are you rounded, all one guardian eye?
> Oh gentlest dark. Gentlest, gentlest night. My darkness.
> My dear darkness . . . .
> Darkness purred with delight . . . .
> And darkness, smiling leaned over more intimately inward upon him, laid open the huge, ragged mouth—[5]

[3] W. M. Frohock, *The Novel of Violence in America* (2nd. ed., Dallas, 1957), 212–30, thinks the novel is unified "poetically," but even Leslie Fiedler, who wrote an otherwise sympathetic review, said that it was "not a completed novel, but a collection of brilliant narrative and lyric fragments given editorially the semblance of a novel." "Encounter With Death," *New Republic*, Vol. CXXXVII (Dec. 9, 1957), 25–26.

[4] See "A Note on this Book, *A Death in the Family* (preceding the contents page).

[5] Page 85.

Perhaps Agee should be given credit for attempting to put into language the emotional experiences of an inarticulate child, but what he produces is merely a pulpy rhetoric that suggests, not a child's emotions so much as an adult's as he leans over the child's crib and gives way to a gush of sentimentality.[6]

At last, then, as a novel, even as a poetic one, A Death in the Family is not first rate; it is a collection of fragments, some of which are quite well written, others of which are not. From the standpoint of past selections, of course, A Death in the Family was a superior choice and must be ranked toward the top of the Pulitzer roster. Perhaps the most remarkable and most gratifying aspect of this selection is that in A Death in the Family, the Pulitzer judges selected a novel that comes to grips with the private experiences of characters that approximate the complexity of human beings.

It was hardly to be expected that, with their oversimplified moral outlook, the Pulitzer authorities would have given serious attention to Vladimir Nabokov's Lolita, even though it was very high on the best-seller lists, and though some reviewers assured their readers that the book did not cater to those with prurient interests.[7] But there were a number of other books available in 1959, the selection of which could not have stirred the mildest scandal. All of these were by young and promising writers of serious fiction: Parktilden Village, by George P. Elliott; Hard Blue Sky, by Shirley Ann Grau; and Magic Barrel, a collection of short

[6] Macdonald, "Death of a Poet," New Yorker, Vol. XXXIII (Nov. 16, 1957), 241, quotes Agee's comment on the film-maker D. W. Griffith and points out that Agee was also describing himself: "He had an exorbitant appetite for violence, for cruelty, and for the Siamese twin of cruelty, a kind of obsessive tenderness which at its worst was all but nauseating . . . ."

[7] Book Review Digest (1958), pp. 792–93.

stories, by Bernard Malamud. The Pulitzer judges, however, succumbed to their recurrent infatuation with stories about the American frontier. They gave the 1959 prize to Robert Lewis Taylor for *The Travels of Jaimie McPheeters.*

Taylor is an accomplished professional writer who has been on the staff of the *New Yorker* magazine for a good many years, and he has turned out a number of readable, urbane works, including biographies of W. C. Fields and Winston Churchill.[8] *The Travels of Jaimie McPheeters* is Taylor's ninth published book and, within the limitations imposed by his subject and form, it is a competent enough achievement. *Jaimie McPheeters* is a picaresque novel, loosely held together by the adventures of the hero. Its subject— the trials and tribulations of a pioneer train moving from Independence, Missouri, to California during the first year of the gold rush—has been exhaustively worked over by popular novelists, Hollywood, and more recently, by television westerns. Despite the triteness of his subject, however, Taylor has managed to fill five hundred and thirty-five pages in such a way that one often fails to notice that he is taking the same route over which less skillful writers have trampled.

The principal virtues of *Jaimie McPheeters* are its somewhat unorthodox tone, the clever blending of styles, and the abundance of and solidity of specification which give Jaimie's adventures a ring of authenticity. Using a boy narrator to somewhat the same advantage as Mark Twain used Huck Finn, Taylor manages to present in a refreshingly ironic light what would otherwise be hackneyed situations. Also, by weaving into the boy's naïve and sometimes simple-minded narrative the letters and journals of his father, Dr. McPheeters, who writes in a florid and self-consciously learned prose, the author provides not only an amusing ironic con-

[8] *New York Times*, May 5, 1959, p. 36.

trast, but he is able unobtrusively to introduce some observations and information that the boy could not be expected to provide.

But *Jaimie McPheeters*, despite its virtues, is not to be taken very seriously. As a review in the *New Yorker* suggested, it is a book to be read for the amusement it provides, for its "cheerful, funny, and headlong prose that makes its unabashed theatricality a total delight," rather than for anything it may have to tell us about the human condition.[9] Taylor subordinates characterization to the exigencies of plot and comes to no conclusions about the meaning or value of his character's experiences, unless one wishes to find a moral in the fact that his emigrants fail to strike it rich in the California gold fields and are obliged to fall back on farming, butchering, and shopkeeping.

Since Pulitzer prizes are given, officially at least, for qualities other than their evocation of amusement, it may be presumed that the Pulitzer authorities regarded this book more seriously than did many of the reviewers. Perhaps some of the judges were impressed by the 140 item bibliography of "principal sources" which Taylor appends to his novel: or perhaps some of them felt, as did Oliver La Farge, a former Pulitzer prize winner (*Laughing Boy*, 1930), that despite some artistic flaws and the concessions to humor and plot, that the book "conveys a real feeling for what it must have been like on the immigrant trails."[10] Considering the Pulitzer authorities' sustained preference for books that give the impression of being firmly rooted in history, it seems quite possible that *The Travels of Jaimie McPheeters* was selected because it was thought to "add another chapter" to the social history of our country.

[9] "Briefly Noted Fiction," Vol. XXXIV (March 22, 1958), 154.
[10] "Fourteen in '49," *Sat. Rev.*, Vol. XLI (April 19, 1958), 23.

It is difficult to believe that the judges who chose *A Death in the Family* or even *Jaimie McPheeters* for Pulitzer prizes would in 1960 ignore John Updike's *The Same Door*, Philip Roth's *Goodbye, Columbus*, Saul Bellow's *Henderson the Rain King*, Faulkner's *The Mansion*, or even Robert Penn Warren's *The Cave*, to select instead *Advise and Consent*, by Allen Drury. But they did. If it is not the least distinguished Pulitzer novel to date, *Advise and Consent* ranks somewhere near the bottom of the roster.[11]

Allen Drury begins his story with the discovery by Robert Durham Munson, who is "Senior United States Senator from the State of Michigan and Majority Leader of the United States Senate," that without consulting him, the President of the United States has nominated Robert Leffingwell, a notorious liberal, to be his Secretary of State. The story moves on through the many repercussions of this nomination, national and international. We overhear coffee conferences of senators and off-the-cuff comments of other politicians; the reactions of reporters; the breakfast table chitchat of the British Ambassador and his wife; the preliminary meeting of the Senate committee to consider the nomination; the hearing of witnesses; the interrogation of the nominee; behind the scenes machinations of the President to force through the confirmation; and so on and so on.

Drury's book is not fiction so much as it is fictitious news. There is little attempt to develop characters. Instead, Drury merely writes *about* them in the clichés of a reporter giving the facts. And as a consequence, his characters are like the figures in an animated waxworks. They resemble people

[11] *Advise and Consent* was a very popular book—not only was it very high on the best-seller lists, it was a Book-of-the-Month selection and a *Reader's Digest* Condensed Book Club selection; it was serialized in newspapers, sold to the movies, and converted into a successful Broadway play. *New York Times*, May 3, 1960, pp. 1, 34.

one recognizes from newspaper photographs and television newsreels. They move and speak. But their movements are always public gestures, and their voices seem to be coming from a sound box rather than from a human throat. Leffingwell, for instance, is simply a figure in a witness chair whom other figures are made to question. The questions are stilted and repetitious, and the answers are long-winded evasions chiefly designed to postpone a shocking "truth" until near the close of the book. The truth turns out to be the long-withheld admission of Leffingwell that, if made Secretary of State, he will never recommend war to the President. This creates a terrible crisis and it becomes clear that Leffingwell must never become Secretary of State.

The whole situation is contrived and totally unconvincing. It is conceivable, of course, that an intellectual might be opposed to war under any circumstances, but it is difficult to believe that a man who feels it necessary to lie about a remote association with the communist party would think it wise— or even necessary—to confess to such war views in public. It is also inconceivable that a President of the United States would nominate such a man to be Secretary of State, and would then stupidly continue to insist on the nomination after it is revealed to him that his nominee had, as Leffingwell had previously, lied to a Senate committee investigating his qualifications. Neither Leffingwell's nor the President's motives are ever gone into. Drury never reveals why Leffingwell is so opposed to war nor why the President is so insistent on having him as Secretary of State. These things are simply introduced as unexplained facts of the novel world.

Most of the novel is a slow setting up of this improbable, unexplained, unexamined situation. Then, toward the close of the book, things happen thick and fast: in order to get Leffingwell's nomination confirmed, Senator Van Ackerman (whose only "motivation," incredible as it may seem, is that he is a "left wing" Joseph McCarthy, a man who "would crawl on his knees to Moscow" to avoid war) threatens to go before his vast radio audience and reveal that Brigham Anderson, the senator chiefly responsible for blocking the nomination of Leffingwell, once engaged in a homosexual relationship. In order to prevent scandal and also to keep Leffingwell from being nominated, Senator Anderson commits suicide. Next, the President is killed off by a heart attack, and the new President is made to appoint Senator Knox, a "conservative" from Illinois, to be Secretary of State. The book is brought to a close as Secretary Knox is about to fly off to Europe where he will take a hard line with the Russians, risking war if necessary to bring back:

> ... a little pinch of accommodation with this enemy so hostile to every human decency in the world; and not necessarily carrying the wealth of the Indies with them, but only a few scraps of things, the memory of a meeting in Philadelphia, a speech at Gettysburg, a few fragments of valor still echoing down the American wind from distant battles and far-off things, Chancellorsville and The Wilderness, The Alamo and San Juan Hill, Belleau Wood and the Argonne, Bataan and Corregidor, Omaha Beach and Salerno, Midway, Iwo Jima, Guadalcanal; a certain way of looking at things, a certain way of living, a form of government that might or might not turn out to be all it was cracked up to be, when all was said and done: on that the final judgment had not yet been rendered ....
>
> So they rode on ... about to learn whether history still had a place for a nation so strangely composed of great ideas and uneasy compromise as she.[12]

As some reviewers pointed out, *Advise and Consent* is a *Roman à clef*, a quality that doubtless made the book doubly

[12] Drury, *Advise and Consent* (Garden City, New York, Doubleday & Co., Inc., 1959), 615–16.

thrilling for many readers.[13] Being able to recognize, for example, the mannerisms, ideologically inverted, of the late Senator Joseph McCarthy behind the villainous Senator Fred Van Ackerman, must have given some readers a sense of intellectual fulfillment and added to their enjoyment of the book's fictitious scandal. Less discerning readers had to be content with just the melodrama, and the scandal, and the vague sense of being in on the dirt about Washington political figures.

This is not to suggest that when Drury wrote *Advise and Consent* that he had scandal-mongering in mind. It is probable that he was as serious about *Advise and Consent* as he tells us he is about his most recent work, *A Shade of Difference*.[14] Drury says he hopes this new novel is widely read because it deals seriously with the "problems of this desperate age." Whether one approves of the way in which the issues raised by *Advise and Consent* are stated, or even whether one believes that the issues so stated are real issues, there is little doubt that behind the sensationalism and the clichés, there are some rather strong, if nebulous, convictions about contemporary politics.

The strongest feeling concerns the dangers of "soft-headed liberalism," which is implicitly defined as always yielding to Russian demands. Leffingwell and Van Ackerman are villains primarily because they are categorically opposed to war. Orrin Knox is heroic mainly because he wants to take a hard line with the Russians. The vast area that lies between these two extremes, the area of reality, is completely ignored. Drury sees the contemporary political world as an international melodrama in which pure white is pitted against

[13] A number of reviewers commented on this quality in the novel. *Book Review Digest* (1959), pp. 301–302.
[14] "What's the Reason Why: A Symposium by Best-Selling Authors," *New York Times*, Dec. 2, 1962, p. 3.

pure black. Moreover, as has been said, the characters in this melodrama never take the shape of credible human beings. One knows, for example, that Seab Cooley (a Southern Senator with whom Drury sympathizes) speaks with an engaging drawl, that he is addicted to certain pet phrases which he repeats over and over, that he joshes the reporters, and that he can be folksy when it suits his purpose. We are told that behind the genial banter, Seab is a tough, shrewd politician, but what Seab thinks on any specific issue, except the nomination of Leffingwell (to which he is unswervingly opposed), is never disclosed. Drury simply describes him—that "fearfully shrewd old man"—in the clichés of journalistic cant. Seab,

> ... carries in his heart a concept of the United States of America that he does not want to see damaged . . . . Mistaken he may be or mistaken he may be not, but at least underneath it all he is as sincere as he has ever been in the long years that stretch out behind him as he moves slowly along with an occasional quick "How you all?" to those in the corridor who interrupt his deep concentration with bright good mornings.[15]

Seab, Drury says, is sincere, and so is to be believed and trusted. One would like to ask whether Leffingwell or Van Ackerman should also be trusted if it could be proved that "underneath it all" they too are sincere? But for Drury *sincerity* here means simply that Seab Cooley is "fiercely faithful to the causes and the friends in which he believes," though who these friends and what these causes are we never learn.

If *Advise and Consent* is an "intellectual discourse," as one reviewer called it, Drury is speaking in the tradition of personality politics.[16] There is not one idea or one issue in

[15] Drury, *Advise and Consent*, 148.
[16] Riley Hughes in the *Catholic World*. See *Book Review Digest* (1959), p. 301.

this novel that ever receives intelligent consideration. Everything is a matter of slogans. Even the matter of what American policy toward Russia should actually be, despite all of the controversy whipped up about it, never gets beyond vague emotional talk about "yielding" and "running away"; in fact, the attitude to be taken toward Russia on international affairs is put by Drury himself on the same level of seriousness as standing up to the neighborhood bully and slugging it out.[17] And, then, after all of the high-sounding talk about sincerity and firmness, the conclusion of the novel—like that of *The Caine Mutiny* and *Andersonville*—seems calculated to please almost everybody by standing nowhere very firmly: on his flight to Europe to meet with the Russians, Orrin Knox's reputed tough-mindedness boils down to the folksy apologetic phrase: all he wants from "this hostile enemy" is "a pinch of accommodation"—hardly the kind of political thinking one would expect from a man who, we are asked to believe, is the great hope of America's future. But no doubt that phrase, "a pinch of accommodation," is Drury's way of reassuring uneasy readers that despite all his reputed combativeness, Orrin Knox is no warmonger. All he wants is one very little concession from the Russians, enough perhaps to show that America is not yellow.

The award to *Advise and Consent*, on the face of it, was a departure from past practices, for the authorities had never before selected a novel that dealt with—or pretended to deal with—current political issues. Now, for the first time, Pulitzer political views were out in the open and these we can see are exactly what might have been anticipated. Pulitzer politics, too, are conservative in the same old sentimental, wooly-

17 See Senator Richardson's speech that begins, "I had rather go out of this world . . . fighting for the things I believe . . ." *Advise and Consent*, 205.

headed way—except that the catchwords and hoary plati-
tudes are expressed in the name of political rather than
economic or "moral" conservatism.

The 1961 award went to another first novel, *To Kill a
Mockingbird*, by Harper Lee. The setting of the novel is a
small Alabama town during the 1930's; the chief character
and narrator is a precocious tomboy named Jean Louise, but
who is called "Scout" by her widower father, her somewhat
older brother, Jem, and by the family servant Calpurnia, who
both mothers and bullies her young charge in the tradition
of the lovable "mammy." The plot is twofold: the first and
minor plot line deals with an eccentric recluse named by the
children "Boo" Radley, whose house is said to be haunted,
and whose shadowy and violent past provides the narrator
and her brother with endless material for speculation and
excitement. Scout's father, Atticus, fails in his attempt to
discourage the children from their preoccupation with this
strange neighbor, Boo Radley, who suddenly and dramatically saves their lives. Then they and the reader learn the
book's moral: that people can be different from you and me
and still be worth-while human beings.

The main plot line is inserted in the middle of the Boo
Radley incident. It makes a similar point, but deals with a
larger social issue, the discrimination against Negroes in the
South. Atticus, a lawyer who serves as the author's voice of
reason and conscience, undertakes to defend a Negro, Tom
Robinson, who has been accused of raping the daughter of a
shiftless poor white. During the trial, it is made clear to even
the lowest intellect in the courtroom that the Negro is innocent. The jury nevertheless finds him guilty. Later he is shot
and killed while trying to escape from a state prison farm.

As a first novel, *To Kill a Mockingbird* is better than

average. Despite its simplistic moral, some early scenes (in the school room especially) are well executed even though they are self-consciously cute. A rather long scene toward the close of the book (the meeting of Aunt Alexandra's church circle) is even more deftly rendered, suggesting that Harper Lee has more talent for writing fiction than a number of more famous Pulitzer winners. But nevertheless, *To Kill a Mockingbird* has major defects. The most obvious of these is that the two plots are never really fused or very closely related, except toward the end when they are mechanically hooked together: the trial is over and Tom Robinson dead, but the poor white father of the girl (whom Atticus had exposed in court as a liar and the attempted seductress of Tom Robinson) swears to get revenge. On a dark night, as they are on their way home from a Halloween party, Scout and Jem are waylaid and attacked by the poor white father. Were it not for the timely interference of Boo Radley, Scout and Jem would be murdered. It is then revealed that, from behind his closed shutters, Boo Radley has all along been watching over the lives of the two children who have been trying to invade his privacy. In addition to her failure to achieve an effective structure, the author fails to establish and maintain a consistent point of view. The narrator is sometimes a mature adult looking back and evaluating events in her childhood. At other times she is a naïve child who fails to understand the implications of her actions. The reason for this inconsistency is that the author has not solved the technical problems raised by her story and whenever she gets into difficulties with one point of view, she switches to the other.

This failure is clearly evident, for instance, during the scene where Scout breaks up a mob of would-be lynchers. This scene is probably the most important section in the novel and it ought to be so convincingly rendered that there will be no doubt in anyone's mind that Scout does the things the author tells us she does. But instead of rendering the actions of Scout and the mob, the author retreats to her naïve point of view. The mob is already gathered before the jail when Scout arrives on the scene. As she looks about, she sees one of her father's clients, Mr. Cunningham, a poor man whose son, Walter, Scout had befriended earlier in the story. When Scout sees Mr. Cunningham she cries, "Don't you remember me, Mr. Cunningham? I'm Jean Louise Finch." When Mr. Cunningham fails to acknowledge Scout's presence, she mentions Walter's name. Mr. Cunningham is then "moved to a faint nod." Scout remarks, "He did know me, after all." Mr. Cunningham maintains his silence and Scout says, still speaking of his son Walter, "He's in my grade . . . and he does right well. He's a good boy . . . a really nice boy. We brought him home for dinner one time. Maybe he told you about me . . . Tell him hey for me, won't you?" Scout goes on in her innocent way to remind Mr. Cunningham that she and her father have both performed charitable acts for him and Walter, and then the mature narrator breaks in and says, "quite suddenly" that Mr. Cunningham "did a peculiar thing. He squatted down and took me by both shoulders. "I'll tell him you said hey, little lady," he says. Then Mr. Cunningham waves a "big paw" at the other men and calls out, "Let's clear out . . . let's get going, boys."[18]

The words "quite suddenly" and "did a peculiar thing" (which are from the point of view of the mature narrator looking back on this scene, and not from that of a naïve little girl as the author evidently wishes us to believe)—these are rhetorical tricks resorted to by fiction writers when they are unable to cope with the difficult problem of rendering a scene

[18] Lee, *To Kill a Mockingbird* (Philadelphia, New York, J. B. Lippincott Co., 1960), 164-65.

dramatically. The author wants Mr. Cunningham to have a change of heart—it is necessary for her story—but she is unable to bring it off dramatically. We are not permitted to *see* Mr. Cunningham change. The author simply reminds *us* that Scout befriended Cunningham's son so that *we* will react sentimentally and attribute *our* feelings to Mr. Cunningham. Further, the author fails to establish (in this scene as well as earlier) that Mr. Cunningham had any influence over the mob *before* Scout arrives on the scene. We do not see the mob react to Mr. Cunningham. Such a reaction, had there been one and had it been well done, might convince us that Mr. Cunningham could lead the mob away simply by waving his big paw. As it is, we have to take Scout's supposed power over Mr. Cunningham's emotions and Mr. Cunningham's remarkable power over the mob—on the author's bare assertion.

A third defect in *To Kill a Mockingbird*, this one inherent in the author's simplistic moral, is her sentimental and unreal statement of the Negro problem. Miss Lee is so determined to have her white audience sympathize with Tom Robinson that, instead of making him resemble a human being, she builds him up into a kind of black-faced Sir Galahad, pure hearted and with a withered right arm. Though the author doubtless did not mean to suggest this, her *real* point is that a good Negro (i.e., a handsome, clean-cut, hard-working, selfless, ambitious, family man who knows his place and keeps to it) should not be convicted of a crime he did not commit. Although it is impossible to disagree with this view, nevertheless it does not seem a very significant position to take in 1961. It seems, in fact, not so very different from the stand of T. S. Stribling in 1933. Stribling defended his Negro's right to rise economically on the emotional grounds that he was *really* a white man.

There will no doubt always be a very large audience in this country for the sub-literary works turned out each year by professional hacks, but over the past two decades popular taste has improved considerably and there is now a fairly large audience for writers whose books would have been read twenty years before only by a handful of discriminating readers. Two obvious examples are J. D. Salinger and John Updike, whose novels and short stories have commanded fairly large audiences and have been highly praised and recommended by popular reviewers.[19] As we have seen, however, the taste of the Pulitzer authorities on the whole has remained at about the same low artistic and intellectual level as it was when prizes were given to Ernest Poole and Booth Tarkington in 1918 and 1919. Thus, in 1962, the authorities again by-passed the work of the most significant younger writers (Salinger's *Franny and Zooey*, Walker Percy's *The Moviegoer*, Carson McCuller's *Clock without Hands*, and Bernard Malamud's *A New Life*) and selected another popular pot-boiler, *The Edge of Sadness*, by Edwin O'Connor.

To many readers, *The Edge of Sadness* is likely to seem a religious book. Indeed, a number of reviewers called it that, and the cover of the paperback edition creates this impression.[20] The narrator *is* a Roman Catholic priest, and much of the novel *does* take place in and around church premises. Also, a number of priests and a bishop are introduced or referred to, and there are even brief discussions of what might in some quarters pass for theological and moral probings. But *The Edge of Sadness* deals only superficially with

[19] Although there were dissenting voices, Salinger's *The Catcher in the Rye, Nine Stories, Franny and Zooey*, and Updike's *The Poorhouse Fair, Rabbit, Run*, and *The Same Door* were highly praised by reviewers in newspapers and popular magazines. See *Book Review Digest* (1951), pp. 772–73; (1953), pp. 821–22; (1961), pp. 1,234–35; and (1959), pp. 1,008–1,009; (1960), pp. 1,366–68.
[20] New York, Bantam Books, 1962.

religious matters. Edwin O'Connor's rectories, priests, and theological questionings are merely part of the misty atmosphere through which the real story and the real issues loom all too clearly.

Father Hugh Kennedy, the narrator, is a reformed alcoholic who has just been assigned to Old St. Paul's, an ancient, decaying parish on the edge of a big-city slum, presumably in Boston. The novel opens with Father Kennedy's returning to the neighborhood where he grew up to attend a birthday party given by Charlie Carmody, father of his boyhood friend, John Carmody, who is also a priest. At first, Father Kennedy is reluctant to return to the old neighborhood after his recent disgrace, but he discovers that he tremendously enjoys old Charlie's birthday celebration, and enjoys talking to the old-timers of Irish descent, especially to Charlie, whom he then continues to see off and on during the next few months. Charlie, it is said, brings back into Father Kennedy's life some of the old color and gaiety that have all but disappeared.

Indeed, it appears that if Father Kennedy has any serious fault, it is in loving the old times and his own people so much that he ignores his parishioners at Old St. Paul's, a miscellaneous congregation of Spaniards, Syrians, Portuguese, Puerto Ricans, and one lone Chinese. Father John Carmody tells Father Kennedy that Old St. Paul's is just a way-station for him on his way back to the place where he, Father Kennedy, really wants to be—St. Raymond's—where Father Carmody is the pastor. Although there is some truth in Father Carmody's observation, it seems that Father Kennedy learns in time to devote himself to his new, heterogeneous flock, and, at the end of the novel, he achieves a kind of sentimental triumph by refusing the Bishop's offer to transfer him to St. Raymond's.

Despite this little triumph, Edwin O'Connor makes it clear that Father Kennedy is a weak man and a sad man, too much given to introspection and a love of privacy. His saving grace is that he realizes the sorry state of his existence and draws sustenance from the abundant vitality of old Charlie, who at eighty-one has all the bounce and energy of a boy of eighteen. Charlie, it seems, has nothing to learn from the Church, but Father Kennedy has a great deal to learn from Charlie, and what he learns, evidently, is responsible for drawing him out of his American-Irish-Catholic niche and into the ecumenical world of Old St. Paul's. Exactly what and how Father Kennedy learns from Charlie and why he finds Charlie's life attractive is never very clear. Charlie is seen at a distance, usually through the neutral camera eyes of Father Kennedy, which show—with Hollywood-like simplicity—a small spry Irishman with a kewpie-doll face, capering about and being, we are assured, very, very droll— rather like the late movie actor, Barry Fitzgerald. Father Kennedy's vision of Charlie amounts to a kind of documentary: Charlie walks wherever he can (instead of riding), collects his own rents, chats with children, priests, tenants, and anyone else who will listen to him. And Father Kennedy finds that even those who profess to hate old Charlie think him a memorable character, a man who has a zest for life.

Although we seldom see Charlie directly, O'Connor does on occasion let us hear Charlie express himself on a number of issues, and what Charlie says seems to suggest that he is not the lovable old rogue Father Kennedy seems to think him. Here, for instance, is a sample from Charlie's famous birthday speech which, we are told, Charlie delivers "easily and with great verve." This speech, it is said, helps draw Father Kennedy back into the old life he used to love:

"So here I am, feelin' grand, and eighty-two . . . . And I can't help but think as I stand here that all over the city and the country too they're chiselin' out tombstones for people younger than me. There's not a day goes by I don't pick up the paper and see where they're sayin' the Dead Mass for someone who was still in knee britches while I was already a married man with a family on the way . . . .

And the little children, too . . . . I'm a great man for the little ones. A soft touch, as they say. Nothin' makes me feel better than to walk over to John's parish school of an afternoon and watch the boys and girls playin' their little games . . . . And what I wonder sometimes," he said, his voice suddenly becoming rather sentimental, "is do they ever think of old Charlie? The way he thinks of them? I wonder do those boys and girls ever stand up by their desks in school, say, and all together recite a little prayer out loud for Mister Carmody? Wouldn't that be lovely? But I don't think they do, I never hear that they do."[21]

Toward the end of the novel, perhaps in despair of making non-Irish readers appreciate Father Kennedy's fondness for Charlie Carmody, we are told that old Charlie brings to Father Kennedy's "calm gray days" a flash of "brightness, an odd bumpy, full-blown boisterousness." In short, Charlie Carmody makes Father Kennedy laugh.[22] Almost everyone in the novel except Father Kennedy and, of course, Charlie (though even he seems to have some doubts about himself) agrees that Charlie Carmody is a tight-fisted, ruthless, unlovable, rent-gouger, who squeezes the lifeblood out of the poor and gives no one anything more substantial than the time of day. Even Charlie's children complain that he is a mean, stubborn, and often vindictive father. Although it is

[21] O'Connor, *The Edge of Sadness* (New York, Little, Brown, 1961), 73–74. (All quotations are from this edition.)
[22] Page 356.

conceiveable that everyone else is wrong about Charlie, O'Connor never makes Charlie's attractive qualities shine through to anyone but his narrator.

To give the author his due, however, he never has Father Kennedy deny that Charlie is a hard-hearted, uncharitable man. In fact, several times, Father Kennedy repeats his own father's remark about Charlie: "There goes as fine a man as ever robbed the helpless." But it is disconcerting to find that Father Kennedy himself is never seriously disturbed by Charlie's rapacity. When Charlie appears to be dying, he calls Father Kennedy to his bedside and begins justifying his past: he has been a hard man, he admits, and is none too proud of some of things he "done," but "by God, Father," he says:

"... life around here was tough. I came out of nothin'; you know that .... And when I was on my way up, d'ye know how many around here gave me a break? Not a soul. Not a livin' soul. But I got up there all the same, and once I did I gave them no more breaks than they gave me. That ain't what the catechism tells us, is it Father? But it's the way I done it. The only way I knew how. And maybe it was bad, I'm not saying it wasn't, but I dunno was it so much worse than what most others were doin'."[23]

Father Kennedy doesn't exactly approve of what Charlie "done," but neither does he disapprove. He simply sits still and, out of compassion or goodness it seems, allows Charlie to defend himself. And then with the kind of intellectual dishonesty, or, more charitably perhaps, incompetence that one frequently encounters in popular fiction, O'Connor glides over the moral issues implicit in Charlie's life: Father Kennedy refuses to pass any judgments on Charlie because:

... for all his faults and misdemeanors and sins—which in any

[23] Page 355.

case, he had now confessed, and which were far out of my jurisdiction—I could only say that what I felt for him, in addition to both affection and pity, was gratitude, a sense of debt. He had given me much, and now I was paying him back; not in full or in kind, but as best I could.[24]

What is it Charlie Carmody gave Father Kennedy besides a hearty laugh and an "odd bumpy full-blown boisterousness" (whatever that is)? By inviting him to his birthday celebration, old Charlie has unwittingly forced Father Kennedy to "face" his own past—his recent bout with alcoholism. But even more important in defending the larger issues of the novel is the other past that Charlie brings back, the "warm recollections of my father and the world in which they both lived—a past, a part of history, of which I'd always been fond . . . ."[25] With this rush of sentimentality, economic and political questions are swept into oblivion— to be joined soon by the moral and religious ones—and Charlie Carmody is revealed in all of his naked symbolism: the real reason he is being held up for our admiration is that Charlie is not just Charlie Carmody. He is the Irish-American version of that familiar Pulitzer hero, the self-made man, the rugged individualist who has raised himself by his own bootstraps: he made money, a great deal of it, and with nobody's help but his own.

The Edge of Sadness is somewhat subtler (or vaguer?) than a number of other Pulitzer prize novels that come to much the same conclusion. Although his style is rather commonplace, O'Connor has learned something about fictional technique from the school of Henry James. He does not, for instance, insist that we admire Charlie Carmody; he turns

[24] Page 373.
[25] *Ibid.*

his narrative over to Father Kennedy and allows us to see Father Kennedy admire Charlie. Instead of functioning as a central intelligence, however, the judgments and evaluations of which we can accept, Father Kennedy is little more than a device for keeping Charlie Carmody out of clear focus during most of the novel. Father Kennedy's priestly office amounts to little more than what students of propaganda call a "transfer" device: since compassionate, sensitive Father Kennedy likes Charlie, is even revived by him and certainly finds nothing reprehensible in his moneygrubbing, the reader, presumably, should like Charlie too and find it regrettable that so many other people, including Charlie's family, find him highly repugnant.

In using Father Kennedy's compassion to defend a man whose life has been a monument to ruthless aggression, the author involves himself in a basic contradiction. For it is not only Charlie whom he admires, but also what Charlie stands for. And, it is one thing to forgive the sinner, but quite another to forgive the sin. Neither Father Kennedy nor his author ever distinguishes between the two, and the reader is asked, on the grounds of compassion, to approve what compassion would require him to reject.

The award given to *The Edge of Sadness*, then, is not so astonishing after all. In giving this book a novel prize, the authorities were not manifesting an alarming inconsistency. They were not embracing Catholicism or even fundamental Christian virtues. Religion—specifically Irish Roman Catholicism—was now very much in vogue, so much so, that instead of a folksy farm wife or a fiery Southern belle, a Pulitzer novelist could now employ Irish drollery and an all too human priest to give the favorite Pulitzer theme of rugged individualism a new coat of whitewash. And so, in 1962, the Pulitzer novel tradition was back in the same old groove it had started in forty-five years ago. The manners of the prize novel were more up to date, of course, and the finish was more highly polished, but the morality was fundamentally the same.

CHAPTER TEN

Conclusion

T HE PULITZER PRIZES are, without doubt, the best-known literary awards in the United States. For many years these prizes have been the subject of an extraordinary amount of publicity—extraordinary at least when compared with the attention paid to other literary awards. The yearly announcement of the prize winners appears on the front pages of newspapers across the country. The *New York Times* and, more recently, the St. Louis *Post-Dispatch* regularly devote two full pages to describing the prize-winning authors and their works. Popular news media, middle-brow literary journals, and some serious political publications fairly regularly report—or used to report—news of the winners and comment on the justness or unjustness of the awards. For a number of years the *Saturday Review* even conducted its own poll of book reviewers in order to compare the results with the outcome of the Pulitzer prize "sweepstakes." Further, the Pulitzer authorities have at times courted public attention by staging impressive award presentation ceremonies which were attended by famous personages (such as General John Pershing), and even by broadcasting the proceedings on a nation-wide radio hook-up; and the prize has been at the center of several spectacular controversies involving well-known writers, faculty members, and high officials of prominent universities. As a result of all this, the Pulitzer prize has become firmly established in the minds of a great many people—including many who never read the prize-winning works—as a badge of indisputable merit. The popular reputation of the Pulitzer prize is such that when a newspaper writer or a television reporter wishes to let his audience know why writers such as William Faulkner and Robert Frost are to be regarded as distinguished, he will invariably invoke the term "Pulitzer prize winner."

However, the most dramatic indications of the public's esteem for the Pulitzer prize are the sales records of the prize-winning novels. Not all of the prize winners sell exceptionally well, of course, but the prize has helped increase the sales of even dullish books by at least a few thousand copies. Also, some livelier works by unknown authors have been converted into best sellers through winning a Pulitzer prize. In 1934, for example, *Lamb in His Bosom* was selling very poorly. Then it won the Pulitzer prize. After that, sales mounted briskly. From 144 copies in the month before the award, sales jumped to 12,936 in the month after the award. During the next month, sales reached 8,000 copies. For a time, *Lamb in His Bosom* was near the top of the best seller list, second to *Anthony Adverse*.[1]

[1] At the end of the year, sales had reached 76,191. In the period before the award, they had amounted to only 6,676, an increase of 69,515. Some other sales statistics on prize novels are: *Honey in the Horn* (1936)—Sales one month before award: none. Sales in month after award: 8,598. Total sales before award: 26,500. Total sales after award: 43,500—an increase of 17,000; *Journey in the Dark* (1944)—Sales one month before award: 733. Sales in month after award: 6,120. Sales in second month after award: 2,479. Total sales before award: 45,250. Total sales after award: 57,600 or an increase of 12,350; *The Able McLaughlins* (1924)—Sales in month award was made: 932. Sales in first month after award: 2,993. Sales second month after award: 2,487. Total sales before award: 38,000. Total sales after award: 54,800—an increase of 16,800; *Arrowsmith* (1926)—Sales before the award: 93,864. Total sales to 1957: 165,940 (Harcourt, Brace and Company could supply only total figures); *In This Our Life* (1942)—Total sales

In addition to the thousands of people who buy novels simply because they were given a Pulitzer prize, uncounted thousands draw these books out of libraries, not only in the months immediately following the award, but for years afterward. Indeed, books that might otherwise be gathering dust in library basements are still circulating because they bear the legend: Pulitzer prize winner. Some libraries encourage the circulation of Pulitzer prize books, not only by prominently displaying the current winners, but also by maintaining on a permanent basis a section of their reading rooms where patrons may quickly locate all the books to which Pulitzer prizes have been given. The implication seems to be that these books constitute an important body of American literature with which all educated people should be familiar.[2]

Nevertheless, despite all this fame, reputation, and audience, it is difficult to locate even one critic who holds the Pulitzer prize in very high repute.[3] In fact, the prize has

before award: 43,547. Total sales to 1957: 45,723—an increase of 2,176; *All the King's Men* (1947)—Total sales before award: 45,845. Total sales to 1957: 51,307—an increase of 5,462. (Sales information was obtained by letter from the publishers.)

Publishers' respect for the Pulitzer prize is also reflected in their use of the label "Pulitzer Prize Winner" in advertisements, and on the covers of reprints. In 1940, after *The Grapes of Wrath* won the prize, Viking prepared a $3,000 advertising campaign. In addition to "large and frequent ads" in the *New York Times* and *New York Herald Tribune*, important space was taken "in twenty-three local papers." See "Pulitzer Prizes Awarded for 1939," *Publ. Wkly.*, Vol. CXXXVII (May 11, 1940), 1846.

[2] The St. Louis Public Library has a special shelf in one reading room on which all the Pulitzer prize novels are located. The Los Angeles Public Library reported that there was no special shelf maintained for the prize winners, but that they frequently were included with "displays of prize novels in general." All the libraries queried have lists of prize-winning books that are readily available to the public.

[3] The Pulitzer drama prize has been the target of a good deal of criticism, especially in the middle 1930's, when New York drama critics founded their own prize as a protest against the Pulitzer awards.

The poetry awards have also been attacked. In 1927, Harriet Monroe

long been condemned. Although there were only a few disgruntled murmurs against the early fiction decisions—idealism was then the avowed standard of the Pulitzer authorities—when the "manners and manhood" requirement was dropped in the 1930's, criticism began to mount. In 1931, an editor of the *New Republic* wrote:

> Viewing the work of the Pulitzer committee as a whole and over the years, it is fair to say that they have been singularly insensitive to the new current sweeping through American writing—that in nearly every instance they have played safe . . . . These committees and their supporters should not be surprised if the prizes are not taken seriously by those who now play the most important part in shaping our literature.[4]

The next year, 1932, S. J. Kunitz, writing in the *New York Tribune* said, "It is no longer a secret that the Pulitzer prize awards mean next to nothing, apart from their dollars-and-cents value to the lucky author."[5] But complaints soon became downright caustic. In 1935, when the Pulitzer authorities passed up several fine novels by established authors (including Fitzgerald's *Tender Is the Night*) and gave the fiction prize to an amateurish work by an unknown young woman, an editor of the *Nation* wrote:

> We cannot see that the prize means very much either to the

---

complained that the decisions were being made by Easterners who were, also, not poets. "Pulitzer Award System," *Poetry*, Vol. XXX (July, 1927), 210–16. Somewhat the same complaint was voiced by Morton D. Zabel in "Use of Prizes," *Poetry*, Vol. L (June, 1936), 154–57.

The history awards were criticized by Bernard DeVoto who reported that the fourteen "leading historians" whom he had asked to select the best books of the past ten years in history (1926–36), "repudiated five of the last ten Pulitzer awards and voted that six of the ten books selected were not 'the best book of the year upon the history of the United States.' " "Pulitzer Prizes in History," *Sat. Rev.*, Vol. XV (March 13, 1937), 3–4.

4 Vol. LXVII (May 20, 1931), 2.

5 As reprinted in *Wilson Lib. Bull.*, Vol. IX (June, 1935), 544.

winners or to the public, and under the circumstances the phraseology of the awards should be modified. Instead of giving the prizes to the "best play," the "best volume" of poems, and so on, the committee should frankly say, "To the play undistinguished enough to meet no objections from either the play jury or the Advisory Board, $1,000."[6]

In the *New Republic* that same year, Malcolm Cowley discussed the merits of the works to which Pulitzer prizes had been given and then offered what he said would be an appropriate speech for Nicholas Murray Butler to give at the prize-awarding ceremonies:

We members of the Advisory Board have great difficulty in making our choices. Individually, some of us are fairly brave, but we begin to quiver and quake as soon as we come together. We are afraid of sex, afraid of ideas, afraid of blood, revolution and coarse language. We are even afraid of the recommendations made by our own committees, which are sometimes careless in tracking down heresies.

Under these circumstances you will understand that it is practically impossible for us to give prizes to the best novel or drama or book of poems. The best in literature always has about it something dangerous. Even the second best is likely to be disturbing, and these prizes are being awarded on the basis of our not having been disturbed. What they really imply is a guarantee to the American public that the two chosen books and the chosen play have nothing in them to shatter conventions or shake the state, nothing to drive the stock market down or interrupt the sleep of virgins.

Pulitzer prize-winners, we had a hard time finding you this year. Some of you we had to take very young, for fear that if we waited too long you would become intellectually troubled and emotionally troubling. We may have a harder time next year, when the battle lines are more clearly drawn. Now as a token

[6] Vol. CXL (May 22, 1935), 589–90.

of our joy in discovery, let us present you with these mid-Victorian Crosses, worth each a thousand dollars. Take them and wear them and let them always remind you that the better part of valor is discretion.[7]

Since 1935, this has remained the attitude of the journals that regularly comment—or used to comment—on the yearly awards.[8] It is also the attitude of literary critics who have made passing references to the Pulitzer prize.[9] Also—and this is even more impressive evidence of the low esteem in which Pulitzer prizes are held by serious literary people—the same attitude, more calmly expressed, is reflected in two fairly long surveys of the prize record, by Arthur Mizener in the *Atlantic Monthly*, and by Carlos Baker in the *Princeton University Library Chronicle*.[10] Both critics treat the prize and the prize givers more dispassionately than had the editors of the *Nation* and the *New Republic*, but both nevertheless conclude that the Pulitzer authorities have clearly failed to select the best fiction published by American writers during the forty-year period covered in their surveys.

7 "The Mid-Victoria Cross," Vol. LXXXVIII (May 22, 1935), 51–52.

8 After Cowley's attack in 1935, there were several more criticisms of the Pulitzer awards in *New Republic*, and then comment in that journal ceased. See: "Lucky Numbers," Vol. XCI (May 12, 1937), 5; "Pooh, pooh Pulitzers," Vol. CIV (May 12, 1941), 653; "Few Sprigs of Laurel," Vol. CVI (May 18, 1942), 653; "Runs, Hits, and Errors," Vol. CVIII (May 17, 1943), 652–53. The editors of *Nation* who also ignored the prize for many years engaged in occasional sniping. See Vol. CLXII (May 18, 1946), 588, and Vol. CXCIV (May 19, 1962), 430. Even the editors of the *Saturday Review* who sometimes defended the prize givers finally gave up their campaign to improve the prize decisions. See especially Vol. VIII (April 23, 1932), 677; Vol. X (May 12, 1934), 688; Vol. XII (May 18, 1935), 8; and Vol. XXV (May 9, 1942), 8.

9 See particularly Charles C. Baldwin, *The Men Who Make Our Novels* (New York, 1924), 428; Fred B. Millett, "Literary Prize Winners," *English Journ.*, Vol. XXIV (April, 1935), 269–82; and Donald Davidson, *The Attack on Leviathan* (Chapel Hill, 1938), 157.

10 Carlos Baker, "Forty Years of Pulitzer Prizes," Vol. XVIII (Winter, 1957), 55–70. Arthur Mizener, "Pulitzer Prizes," Vol. CC (July, 1957), 42–45.

Today, the attitude of all judicious critics toward the prize is almost automatic. Attacks have been made, no improvements seem to have resulted, and critics have more or less washed their hands of the Pulitzer prize. The general consensus is in agreement with Mr. Mizener and Mr. Baker— that the Pulitzer authorities have consistently passed over the best and most significant novels of our time. The truth of this charge can be quickly verified by examining the record. Before 1952 not one of the major American novelists of this century received a Pulitzer prize, although all were eligible more than once. Dreiser, Anderson, Dos Passos, Fitzgerald, Hemingway, and Faulkner head the list of those whose books were repeatedly ignored by the Pulitzer prize givers. Since 1952, Hemingway and Faulkner have received prizes, but only after having established popular and widespread critical acceptance. Their prize-winning books, moreover, were clearly inferior to their earlier, more controversial work. It is quite evident that the Pulitzer authorities have made a practice of getting belatedly onto the band wagon.[11]

In the face of such an obvious failure on the part of the Pulitzer authorities to keep abreast of the best American fiction, and in the face of the endless criticism to which they have been subjected, one might ask why some effort has not been made to improve the quality of the Pulitzer decisions. The answer is not far to seek: the Pulitzer authorities have never recognized the need for improvement. The yearly announcement that such and such a novel was "the best" or

[11] Against the Pulitzer record must also be charged the neglect of a great number of important American writers: Thomas Wolfe, Caroline Gordon, Nathanael West, James T. Farrell, Eudora Welty, Carson McCullers, Peter Taylor, Kay Boyle, J. F. Powers, Jean Stafford, Saul Bellow, J. D. Salinger, Flannery O'Connor, Philip Roth, John Updike, and a number of lesser-known but talented men and women whose books were eligible in years when much inferior works were chosen.

the "distinguished" novel of the year has not been made reservedly, as the critics imply when they suggest that the Pulitzer authorities have been guided by timidity and fear of controversy. The Pulitzer prize novels were chosen, not just because they were popular and non-controversial. They were chosen because they embodied qualities that the Pulitzer judges found attractive.

Assuming that this is true—and there is little reason for thinking otherwise—let us summarize the aggregate standard of the Pulitzer juries. Basic to the Pulitzer judges' taste, certainly, has been the requirement that the prize work tell a "rattling good story," or, as one official announcement put it, that the prize fictional work "sustain interest."[12] Critics whose interest is engaged only by novels that are artistically and intellectually complex often forget that what chiefly interests non-literary people in the novel is simply the narrative excitement. This interest, in part at least, lies behind the frequent selection of works that have lingered at the top of the best-seller lists for so many months, such fabulously popular works as, for example, *Gone With the Wind* and *The Caine Mutiny*. These books might, of course, have been given Pulitzer prizes even if they had not been popular, since the authorities also value qualities other than excitement.

One of these other qualities looked for in Pulitzer prize fiction is timeliness. The prize novel has to deal—or appear to deal—with a problem that seems to the Pulitzer jurors to be a burning public issue. As we have seen, the jurors' concern over the years has frequently been with the issue of rugged individualism. And a common assumption of all the novels dealing with this subject is that virtue inheres in

12 Part of the official statement made in explanation of the award to *The Store* (1933). "Pulitzer Awards Announced," *Publ. Wkly.*, Vol CXXIII (May 6, 1933), 1,475.

physical toil and in the attempt to lift one's self by one's own bootstraps into a higher economic stratum. In the novels that treat this issue there is usually this question raised: how rugged should rugged individualism be? Different novels present different answers, depending upon the bias of the author and current social and economic conditions. Some Pulitzer novels condemn cutthroat business practices and some romanticize the ruggedest forms of rugged individualism.

During the early years, except for Booth Tarkington's snobbery in *Alice Adams* (those who have money deserve to have it, and those who do not ought to work hard and enjoy their poverty), Pulitzer novels showed homey examples of how ingenuity, determination, and hard work solved life's problems, and brought money and beauty into the worker's life. Money that was obtained too easily or dishonestly was shown to be both a cause and a symbol of corruption. Later, during the late 1920's and the early 1930's, the Pulitzer prize-givers' interest was sustained chiefly by problems of drinking, sexual promiscuity, and related vices (Bohemianism, art-for-art's sake, etc.). Some Pulitzer novels in these years, before the effects of the depression were felt very deeply, continued to lay the blame for soft living on the possession of too much easy money, although an added factor sometimes was that people were abandoning the farm and migrating to the corrupt cities. By the middle of the 1930's, however (when some American farmers were actually starving on the land), the new solution was faith in the hills and hope that somehow everything would turn out all right.

A number of Pulitzer novels, of course, do not deal with present events at all, but with the American past. This past, as represented in Pulitzer fiction, is frontier America around the time of the Civil War, a land then peopled by a race of giants who are shown to be physically and morally superior (i.e. more self-reliant) to those who came after them. These great, but humbly simple folk are able to survive calamities that would drive an ordinary mortal to the brink of madness or, at the least, to the edge of exhaustion. But Pulitzer pioneer types ask nothing better than the opportunity to labor on the frontier or to fulfill America's manifest destiny. To be sure, some of them grow rich, but their riches really seem to be an accident and they would not think of spending money ostentatiously. In the midst of their wealth, they remain plain American folks, satisfied with their unstylish clothes, their lusterware, and their humble rag carpets. The children of these virtuous folk, however, are another matter. Invariably they lack their parents' gumption and get-up-and-go, and they are shown by their authors to be pretty sorry, unself-reliant specimens.

Although women have evidently not served on the Pulitzer fiction juries, it is interesting to note that there has been a fairly consistent preference for fiction oriented toward what might be called middle-class female wish fulfillment. The protagonists of Pulitzer novels are very often sweet but aggressive women who are married to weak, ineffectual, and usually stupid men. For a time they are dominated by their husbands or hemmed in by the genteel manners and prejudices of their time, both of which prevent them from standing on their own more than capable feet. But when they are forced to do so by circumstances beyond their control, they heroically shake off the role of the passive female and assume a more dominant and aggressive position at home and in their community. They become shrewd farmers, successful operators of businesses, and, in general, the moral guide, teacher, and mainstay of a world unsuccessfully run by men. Sometimes, as a final reward, the Pulitzer heroine at about the age of sixty-five is provided with a younger man who adores and sometimes marries her. There may occasionally be male tycoons, respected artists, or a dedicated scientist in Pulitzer novels, but the successful and admirable male is usually a minor character, a foil to the more successful female. The typical Pulitzer protagonist is somewhat womanish, weak, timid, fearful of change, nervous, afraid of work, ineffectual, and given to feeling sorry for himself and other unfortunates. On the rare occasions when a Pulitzer hero asserts his masculinity, he is usually killed off or forced to knuckle under to polite female-dominated society.

But whether the hero of a Pulitzer novel is a man or a woman (or an effeminate man or a masculine woman), the personal qualities chiefly celebrated in these works are self-reliance, industriousness, and acquisitiveness (sexlessness is often a corollary). With the emphasis on these attributes, it is not surprising to find Pulitzer men and women involved in a kind of inhuman drama in which love and money, virtue and business success are inextricably twined. Indeed, the equation of money-getting with virtue is so frequent in Pulitzer prize fiction that if one took at face value the original conditions under which Pulitzer fiction prizes were given, one would have to conclude that for the Pulitzer authorities, the highest standard of American manners and manhood is little more than sublimated greed.

The art of Pulitzer fiction, as we have seen, is frequently crude, sometimes laughably so. Instead of a reasonably complex illusion of human experience, the Pulitzer author usually presents a black-and-white world in which the bad guys are defeated and the good guys come out on top. And there is seldom any doubt about which is which. It would be a mistake, of course, to assume that the issues raised in these novels and the view of life they present can be entirely dismissed. In a very real sense, the Pulitzer prize novels are closer to what are commonly called the "realities" of American life than are the novels of much better writers. For to the evident satisfaction of a great many readers besides the Pulitzer judges, these prize novels dramatize what are taken to be deeply significant truths about life. Success in practical affairs, making the right kind of impression, having the right kind of house, car, and furnishings—these are not just the materials with which Pulitzer novelists deal. These are also, it would seem, the gauges by which the moral worth of the individual is to be tested.

The morality of most Pulitzer prize fiction—practical, down-to-earth, realistic—whether one likes it or not, is shared by a good many people, not only thoughtless readers of best sellers, but people who think of themselves as intelligent, perhaps even intellectual, conservatives, and who dislike what they think of as the nihilism and the futilitarianism of so many modern works of fiction. Some of these conservatives see novels such as *One of Ours*, *Guard of Honor*, and even *Gone With the Wind* as answering and perhaps even combating the destructionistic tendencies of writers like Fitzgerald, Hemingway, and Faulkner.[13] Much as one might wish that the Pulitzer authorities had exercised better judgment over the past forty-five years, it is nevertheless useful to us that they have brought together under one banner so many novels that vigorously assert a popular American attitude.

[13] This particular brand of literary conservatism has not had many articulate apologists. Edward Wagenknecht, whose comments on *Gone With the Wind* have already been quoted (Chapter V above) is perhaps best known and most widely respected. See *Cavalcade of the American Novel* (New York, 1952), particularly Chapter XXIII, "A Note on the Fiction of the 'Forties and After," pp. 449–64. More recently, John Lydenberg has attempted to distinguish between mature, intellectually respectable conservatives like James Gould Cozzens and the sentimentalizers of middle-class respectability like Herman Wouk, in "Cozzens and the Conservatives," *Critique*, Vol. I (Winter, 1958), 3–9.

Not only are we able to watch this so-called conservative point of view as it alters over the years, but also we are permitted to see in each case exactly why such a view of life fails to produce successful art. For although it is a truism, Pulitzer prize novels illustrate, most of them negatively, that art and morality do indeed lie very close together.

Index

The Pulitzer Prize Novels has been cast on the Linotype in eleven-point Electra, a type called "modern" but possessing transitional characteristics. It has highly appropriate overtones for a subject so clearly identified with the twentieth century. Electra's clean charm of design, enhanced by the classic beauty of Deepdene Italic and Michelangelo display, lends distinction to any printed page. The paper on which this book has been printed is designed for an effective life of at least three hundred years.

UNIVERSITY OF OKLAHOMA PRESS
NORMAN